CLERGYMEN
OF THE
CHURCH OF ENGLAND

THE VICTORIAN LIBRARY

CLERGYMEN
OF THE
CHURCH OF ENGLAND

ANTHONY TROLLOPE

WITH AN INTRODUCTION BY
RUTH apROBERTS

LEICESTER UNIVERSITY PRESS

1974

First published in volume form in 1866
Victorian Library edition published in 1974 by
Leicester University Press

Distributed in North America by
Humanities Press Inc., New York

Introduction copyright © Leicester University Press 1974

Printed in Great Britain by
Unwin Brothers Limited, The Gresham Press
Old Woking, Surrey

ISBN 0 7185 5023 4

THE VICTORIAN LIBRARY

There is a growing demand for the classics of Victorian literature in many fields, in political and social history, architecture, topography, religion, education, and science. Hitherto this demand has been met, in the main, from the second-hand market. But the prices of second-hand books are rising sharply, and the supply of them is very uncertain. It is the object of this series, THE VICTORIAN LIBRARY, to make some of these classics available again at a reasonable cost. Since most of the volumes in it are reprinted photographically from the first edition, or another chosen because it has some special value, an accurate text is ensured. Each work carries a substantial introduction, written specially for this series by a well-known authority on the author or his subject, and a bibliographical note on the text.

The volumes necessarily vary in size. In planning the newly-set pages the designer, Arthur Lockwood, has maintained a consistent style for the principal features. The uniform design of binding and jackets provides for ready recognition of the various books in the series when shelved under different subject classifications.

Recommendation of titles for THE VICTORIAN LIBRARY and of scholars to contribute the introductions is made by a joint committee of the Board of the University Press and the Victorian Studies Centre of the University of Leicester.

CONTENTS

INTRODUCTION

In January 1866 Anthony Trollope set to work to write *The Last Chronicle of Barset*, having proved himself, that is, in a fictional clerical world and now with that word *Last* seeming to suggest that he had exhausted the vein or at least was determined on a change. In the preceding months he had paused in his novel-writing to do some little essays for the *Pall Mall Gazette* where he capitalized on his expertise, essays best described as 'characters' or 'types', of "Clergymen of the Church of England". He had done something the same for the same paper with "Hunting Sketches" – "The Lady who Rides to Hounds", "The Hunting Parson", and so on; and "Travelling Sketches" – "The Unprotected Female Tourist", "The Art Tourist", and so on; and I think he had profited from practice, and while the other sketches all have interest these last have a particular polish and distinction that relate them to the Theophrastian genre. The 'character' is not a particularly Victorian mode. One remembers George Eliot's satirical *Impressions of Theophrastus Such* (1879), but barely. Thackeray's *Snobs*[1] fit the genre in some ways, and

are certainly memorable, but Trollope's sketches are
more the traditional 'character', being more discrete,
and somewhat more charitable and gentle in their
satire. They owe something of their tone to the paper
where they were published. The *Pall Mall Gazette*
was originally a fiction of Thackeray's, in *Pendennis*
(1849–50), a paper "by gentlemen for gentlemen";
it became real in 1865 two years after Thackeray's
death, and Trollope was a frequent contributor.[2]
Admirer of Thackeray's that he was, he maintains
here some of what Thackeray admired, the grace of
the eighteenth-century periodical essay: its *nil
admirari*, its urbanity, combined with a perfectly
serious moral bias. He excels at the laconic style, the
well-turned sentence with a little surprise in it that
represents some close observation. "In the religion of
today, moderation is everything". "The parish
parson generally has a grievance, and is much
attached to it . . .". "We love our old follies infinitely
better than our new virtues".

The genre is by no means foreign to Trollope's
novels; in fact these portraits can serve to remind us
how Trollope generally excels at the portrait, usually
minor characters presented with a terse economy.
Even major characters make their entrance this way;
it will be something like caricature at first, and then
as the story proceeds the caricature takes on the light
and shade of reality. The well-read Trollopian will
recognize this process incipient in the *Clergymen*; one
feels that if Trollope were to stay longer with these

characters there would be novelistic situations developing around them, demanding three-volume-size exploitations.

A reprint of the *Clergymen* essays may be welcomed then, for itself and for its relevance to Trollope's art. But there is a value here more than literary. The changes of the nineteenth century seem worth our close study, and may somehow help us understand and define our own times. Our new interests in cultural anthropology and comparative religions make us freshly curious about the Victorians now we have got through reacting and despising. What was it that happened to the peculiar institution of an Established Church? How could it all have mattered so much? What made it matter, and what has made it matter less? How did it work, and what kind of men officiated? Novels are great resources for sociology, of course, and Trollope's especially so because he interests himself in the interplay of principle and actual practical exigency. Owen Chadwick in his *The Victorian Church*[3] refers to Trollope *passim* for ecclesiastical actualities. There is only one impossibility in *Barchester Towers*, he says (I, 473) – the appointment by Palmerston of a Tractarian to the deanery (he means Arabin, of course). Trollope's novels evince repeatedly – it is their most recurring concern – the insistence on the practical as opposed to the theoretical. He exemplifies what a later school of Anglican thinking has called 'situation ethics', and that is why, I think, the novels are of interest to us today, as cases, as situations, the forum where ethical systems are obliged to apply themselves. Life obliges us to be practising psychologists and moralists; we are all *behavers* and like to think we do not move at random. Yet Trollope's novels are novels and not mere case histories, and we are luckier for that. In fact they are so successful as novels that we are inclined to slight the considered ethical position in which they are based. These essays on Clergymen fall into a special category, somewhere between abstraction and realistic fiction. They lean toward abstraction in that because of its generalization each can demonstrate the nature of the Church, the office, and men's attitudes. The abstractions are made accessible because of the character's specificity: they are possible people. Because of our incurably anthropomorphic turn of mind, we can learn much of trends and tendencies through these characters – who, because they are Trollope's, keep trying to turn real.

There is yet another reason why these Clergymen are to the point just now. Trollope has always been read, but it is only lately that he has been granted the dignity of serious theoretic analysis. Our theories – Jamesian, Joycean, Leavisite, formalist – have not been much help with Trollope (or Tolstoy, for that matter). We want now to see where the art of it consists; we cannot any longer dismiss him as a mere artless sort of photographer of the ordinary. To help determine the principles of his art, the novels are certainly the prime exhibit, but let us look afresh at his *Autobiography* and *Letters*, too; at his criticism – essays, lectures, magazine pieces. These Clergymen essays may be particularly important, offering at times the discursive formulation of many ideas and attitudes that shape his art. For instance, if Trollope sees his office like that of clergymen – "the novelist, if he have a conscience, must preach his sermons with the same purpose as the clergyman, and must have his own system of ethics"[4] – we had better see how he conceived the purpose of the clergyman, and systems of ethics. "The Parson of the Parish" (v) defines these things more specifically, I think, than any of his other writings. His political views even are often elegantly explicit here. Although the essays are almost as diverting as his fiction, they reveal his principles better just because they are not fiction.

It seems surprising at first, for an author who writes so much about the clergy and politicans and lawyers, about what seem to be actual affairs, that one is puzzled to define his position. In the notoriously partisan battles of the Age of Reform, ecclesiastical, political and social, where does Trollope stand? To George Eliot, he seemed to be "a Church of England man, clinging to whatever is, on the whole."[5] Certainly we do not catch the note of the propagandist-reformer in his work. Yet, politically, he called himself an "advanced Conservative-Liberal" (*Autobiography*, 243), and when he stood for election it was as a Liberal. Perhaps whatever is, on the whole, or *was* in the 1860s, was an assumption that reform was the state of things; and so to stand for the status quo was to accede to change, but – in the English style – to recommend moderation in the rate of change. Meanwhile, Trollope as detached artist withdraws to present situations which demonstrate the case for moderation. His moral dilemmas demonstrate that no strong line can be applied to all cases. What else is *The Warden* but such a demonstration? John Bold is right, Tom Towers is right, and Septimus Harding is – not right, but he is a saint. It is best to describe Trollope's position as partisan only insofar as he is in favour of social justice and righteousness. Otherwise he is non-partisan, anti-theroretical, anti-systematic, anti-dogmatic. It is for this reason that I have called him elsewhere a *casuist* in the good sense, a practitioner of *situation ethics*, and have suggested that he thereby stands within a certain Anglican tradition.[6] Consequently, when he says the novelist has the same purpose as a clergyman, and must have his own system of ethics, we may gloss with some certainty: the purpose is not to promulgate dogma, but to enlarge our understanding of the varieties of conduct, to help us recognize right conduct, according to the principles of charity, to help us to know when to condone and imitate, and when to deplore and anathematize. That is not quite all. He reveals the rest when he writes of Thackeray, who was always, he says,

   'crying his sermon', hoping, if it might be so, to do something toward lessening the evils he saw around

> him. . . . He had become so urgent in the cause, so
> loud in his denunciations, that he did not stop often
> enough to speak of the good things around him.
> Now and again he paused and blessed amid the
> torrent of his anathemas.[7]

Trollope feels the act of *blessing* is the office of the
novelist. Perhaps most admirers of Trollope would
agree that he does succeed in this benign office. To
define it, is to come up against something of religious
mystery, but even the least mystically inclined would
grant that there is a base in psychological actuality.

This is about as close to anything like orthodox
Christian supernaturalism that Trollope allows himself
to come. In general, his religious principles are quite
surprisingly close to those of another distinguished
Victorian who is very remote from him in most ways,
and I think the likeness needs remarking, as Trollope
has been so often thought simplistic and commonplace. The whole weight of Trollope's novels leans
toward the dismissing of matters of dogma and
theology as non-essential. What matters is conduct.
Is this not precisely the central point of Matthew
Arnold's views on religion? Trollope habitually
deflates man's rationality, using quite frequently the
locution "he thought that he thought", and considering that if *belief* and *faith* are themselves rather
difficult of definition, they cannot in fact be the main
issue. Note below in Essay x, "It is very hard to
come at the actual belief of any man." Even for our-

selves, it is hard to say what we *believe*. "Not very
many clergymen even . . .".

It is my experience that one tends to read the
periodicals one publishes in oneself, and it happens
that Arnold was a standby contributor to the *Pall
Mall Gazette*, even in the same years Trollope was.
Although I know of no place where Trollope refers to
Arnold, I think he knew his work. There seems from
the first to have been a basic similarity in religious
stance, but it is later that I think we can find evidence
of some actual Arnoldian influence. This is in *The Way
We Live Now* (1873) when Arnold had formulated the
ideas of *Culture and Anarchy*, *Paul and Protestantism*
and *Literature and Dogma*. There is in *The Way We
Live Now* (Chapter xvi, especially) a pair of exem-
plary clergymen who could be demonstrations of
Arnold's point. One is Father Barham, a Roman
Catholic priest, a convert, and the most zealous of
proselytizers – and dogma-ridden. "The dogmas of
his Church were to Father Barham a real religion . . .
Faith being sufficient . . . moral conduct could be
nothing to a man, except as a testimony of faith."
The other is the Anglican Bishop. "Perhaps there was
no bishop in England more loved or more useful in
his diocese than the Bishop of Elmham." Father
Barham becomes so impossible that one can simply
no longer have him as a friend; he is unfit for social
intercourse. It is not to be gathered from this that
Trollope is anti-Catholic or anti-priest. He has in
fact remarkably sympathetic and respectful pictures

of Catholic priests, from the early *McDermots of Ballycloran* in 1847 to the late *An Eye for an Eye* in 1879. Of course it is almost too obvious to say that not all his Anglican clergy are ideal, but with these two clergymen, one is certainly deplored and the other condoned, and the point is the relation of dogma to conduct. As for the Bishop,

> Among the poor around him he was idolized, and by such clergy of his diocese as were not enthusiastic in their theology either on one side or on the other, he was regarded as a model bishop. By the very high and the very low,—by those rather who regarded ritualism as being either heavenly or devilish,—he was looked upon as a time-server, because he would not put to sea in either of those boats.

It is interesting that Trollope defended Cicero from the charge of equivocation and found him a hero, for his flexible *humanitas;* and Arnold in a somewhat parallel way defends Falkland from the same charge and finds him proof that moderation is consistent with strength and honour and religion. Trollope's bishop

> was an unselfish man, who loved his neighbour as himself, and forgave all trespasses, and thanked God for his daily bread from his heart, and prayed heartily to be delivered from temptation. But I doubt whether he was competent to teach a creed, —or even to hold one, if it be necessary that a man

should understand and define his creed before he
can hold it. Whether he was free from, or whether
he was scared by, any inward misgivings, who shall
say? If there were such he never whispered a word
of them even to the wife of his bosom . . . He was
diligent in preaching,—moral sermons that were
short, pithy, and useful.

He was tireless in good works, "but he was never
known to declare [like Father Barham] to man or
woman that the human soul must live or die forever
according to its faith." There was in Victorian times
what we might call an excessive honesty in religious
matters, due no doubt to the literalism Arnold deplored.
Arnold's own brother Tom seems over-conscientious
in his frequent conversions to and away from Rome.
But here is Trollope's bishop, who may have had
"doubts" but never told anyone! Arnold declares a
clergyman, even, "may honestly be silent" when he is
unsure on doctrine.[8] His silence is better for his
congregation than his honesty would be. The irony of
Trollope's last essay here, is that the clergyman must
declare himself on doctrine, must either subscribe for
Colenso or not subscribe, and yet this matter has
really nothing to do with the proper discharge of his
duty.

In *The Way We Live Now*, Trollope has been considered to take a more serious tone than elsewhere. I
think that even here he maintains his characteristic
ironic detachment. Lady Carbury once had spoken to

the Bishop of her soul, thinking defensibly enough that this was the province of the man of God. However, "The first tone of the good man's reply had convinced her of her error, and she never repeated it." Trollope maintains his breadth of sympathy even for popish saints! Father Barham "was endless in prayer, wearying the saints with supplications." Actually, Barham and the Bishop are comparatively non-essential to the novel, and it would seem that the Arnoldian line of thinking is so germane to Trollope's that he gratuitously objectifies it in these two interesting and non-essential clergymen. He even has the Bishop speak in very Arnoldian terms of the collapse of the Roman empire and the beginnings of Christianity.[9] At any rate, Roger Carbury, who was playing host to both men, was himself "not a man given to much deep thinking, but he felt that the Bishop's manner was the pleasanter of the two." Thus, at bottom, it is this anti-dogmatic position of Trollope's that makes his detachment possible, and he can see the strife of party and faction in the church as ephemeral. For him, the secret of ethics is something the pagan Cicero had, almost as well as ourselves, in *honestum* and *humanitas*. With Christ, however, we have come farther; with "to do unto others. . ." we have "the rudiments of that religion which has served to soften the hearts of us all."[10] And hence Trollope can look with so detached and yet so loving an eye on the workings of institutionalized religion.

He writes so knowingly. Yet he tells us in the *Autobiography* (78):

> No one . . . could have had less reason than myself to presume himself to be able to write about clergymen. I have often been asked in what period of my early life I had lived so long in a cathedral city as to have become intimate with the ways of a Close. I never lived in any cathedral city,— except London, never knew anything of any Close, and at that time had enjoyed no peculiar intimacy with any clergyman. My archdeacon . . . was, I think, the simple result of an effort of my moral consciousness.

He did not know the Church, then, but he knew another branch of the Establishment very well indeed – he knew the Post Office. He knew the clash of personality and the stresses of hierarchy, the demands of expediency, the accommodation of principle to practice, the problems of righting inequities in an age of reform, of adjusting to political realities and patronage and the spoils system; he knew how men scrounge and jockey for place and advantage, and yet how they do manage finally to work together, and how the service is done – and done well on the whole, Trollope felt, with some pride. This success of the Civil Service, Trollope explains, depends in good measure on recruitment from among "gentlemen" (*Autobiography* 32–3); a similar idea was quite standard in the Church of England – so much so that

Hurrell Froude wittily referred to the *gentleman-heresy*. Trollope would certainly be a heretic of this party. For him especially the *gentleman* is a moral ideal, Ciceronian and practical.

In all these respects, it will seem, perhaps, that the Anglican Church is another branch of the Civil Service. Trollope was able to evoke actual personalities in one branch because he knew so much of Organization Man in general. He did so well with his imaginary journalist Tom Towers of *The Jupiter* that a critic in *The Times* rebuked him for "indulging in personalities" (*Autobiography* 83–4), and at that time he was living in Ireland and had no knowledge of anyone connected with *The Times*. So strong was what he calls simply his "moral imagination". We call it artistic imagination and are reminded once again of the interdependence in Trollope between art and morals. We recognize his sure sense of artistic irony in dealing with the clergy. For here, because of the special nature of the Organization, its high office, and its supernatural claims and its heavenly connections, here the natural and earthly man shows in the sharpest relief. There is nothing really irreverent in this, either. Wise churchmen have always been careful to distinguish between man and office. In dealing with an organization that professes charity and forgiveness, and in its Anglican form a special brand of tolerance, Trollope himself exercises that tolerance and loving acceptance that are sometimes considered to be Christian virtues.

In general terms, then, Trollope takes the long view, and this has something to do with art, and suggests why the novels can still be valid when the issues are dead. Nevertheless to know the contemporary issues helps in understanding the novels and these sketches. When in 1866 he writes these sketches he has come far from the state of ecclesiastical innocence of 1852–3 in which he wrote *The Warden*. Certainly he now knew many clergymen, and in this time when religious and ecclesiastical matters were of great public interest anyway, he certainly knew the state of things. By the 1860s many issues had become clear: the dramatic part of the Oxford Movement was over, the Christian Socialist movement was no longer news, the Ecclesiastical Commission, established in 1836, was accepted as the continuing agent of reform, and as P. T. Marsh puts it, there was "a period of balanced tensions."[11] There was enough stability for Trollope to exercise his sociological sense of types, and there had been certain landmarks that helped – as it were – to draw up the lines of controversy. *The Origin of Species*, making the scientific challenge especially clear, was published in 1859. In 1860 came *Essays and Reviews*, articulating the challenge of liberalism and the Higher Criticism. Then it was in 1862 that Colenso published the first and most controversial part of his commentary on the Penta-teuch. The Colenso case gave Trollope just the sort of moral dilemma he characteristically uses for the *donnée* of a novel. Essay x takes up this dilemma.

It is the most topical of the sketches. In general, there are remarkably few topicalities, and what follows here are what one might want by way of explanation of references to actual people and events, and some review of analogues in Trollope's fiction.

I. The Modern English Archbishop

Trollope does not have any archbishops in his fiction; as he says, archbishops should not make themselves too common, and so they could be admonished, it would seem, to keep out of novels. To talk about the archbishop here is an occasion to epitomize the anomalies of English reform, the Victorian compromise, and the middle-ness of the Via Media itself. "We hate an evil, and we hate a change. Hating the evil most, we make the change but we make it as small as possible." How Trollopian a political situation it is, the difficulty of Prime Ministers in selecting an archbishop, who "must seem to control, and yet not control", be "great enough . . . and yet small enough", and must stay that way, for once chosen, he is there for good, and so "must remember that quiescence for which credit was given him when he was chosen." With bishops, we can have High and Low and Broad, a variety of commitments, counterbalancing various men, just as they were chosen by various ministries. But an archbishop is a master "of words which may mean as little as words can be made to mean, and carefully watching that he commit himself to nothing."

This may seem harsh; and yet Trollope shows an affectionate respect for this ideal of equivocation. Perhaps it *can* demand respect. It sorts well with the spirit of ecumenicism which we find admirable enough in these days – Trollope's archbishop is friends both with Dissenters and Roman Catholics. It may be merely wishy-washy; but Rose Macaulay thought it one of the strengths of the Anglican Church – "Less certainty, more scope." The author of the article on the Thirty-nine Articles in the *Oxford Dictionary of the Christian Church* explains, "Though not ostensibly vague, they avoid unduly narrow definition", and Article 17, concerning predestination, he declares to be *masterly* in its *ambiguity*. Ambiguity is an Anglican specialty.

As for the historicity of the portrait: Trollope mentions only one real name – Longley, who was Archbishop of York 1860–2, of Canterbury 1862–8. For an actual analogue of the character, William Howley might serve best. Although a little early for Trollope's essay – he was Archbishop of Canterbury 1828–48 – he was so typical for so long that I think he stands behind the Trollopian image. Consider these selections from the index of Chadwick's *Victorian Church* under *Howley*: "against reform bill . . . proposes fast . . . praises Methodists . . . refuses to let Arnold preach [the heretically Broad Thomas, of course, father of Matthew] . . . agrees to renew Ecclesiastical Commission . . . gentle with cathedral reform . . . liked by everyone . . . wears wig . . . confused at queen's coronation . . . at first disliked later beloved by queen . . . confused at queen's marriage . . . subscribes to martyrs' memorial . . . wishes *Tracts* stopped . . . confused at prince's baptism [apparently there was some fear that he would drop the infant] . . . draws attention of Peel to atheist pamphlets . . . quietens surplice riots . . . advises withdrawal of suit . . . alleged to approve union with R. C.s . . . not a good speaker . . . death . . . memory revered."

It was under Howley that the Ecclesiastical Commission was formed, in 1835. Clearly the Church had to be both reformed and placated, and Peel's idea was that reform be proposed "not by government but to government by a commission of responsible churchmen" (Chadwick, I, 103). Howley chose the clergy, Peel chose the laymen. Churchmen, says Chadwick, "were confident in Howley's power of braking and wished he looked a little fiercer." Anyway, reform proceeded *à l'anglaise*, slow and by degrees, that affair of Hiram's Hospital was put to rights, and the Ecclesiastical Commission has continued to manage the estates and revenues of the Church of England to this day, being slightly reconstituted only as late as 1948.

II. *English Bishops, Old and New*

For the Old, here, Trollope takes the days "in which Lord Eldon was first consulted as to the making of a bishop" – this is that John Scott (1751–1838), first Earl of Eldon, Lord Chancellor under George IV to whom he was affectionately known as "Old Bags", highly conservative and very powerful in the dispensing of patronage; and the New is the recent years "in which bishops are popularly supposed to have been selected in accordance with the advice of a religious Whig nobleman" – this is Shaftesbury, connected by marriage to the Prime Minister Lord Palmerston. Shaftesbury was initially disquieted by what he considered Palmerston's incompetence in ecclesiastical appointments: "He does not know, in theology, Moses from Sydney Smith"; but as it turned out Palmerston had the great good sense to be guided by the anti-Puseyite Shaftesbury. Bishop Proudie's appointment to the see of Barchester was the sort of thing that resulted.

Trollope notes that, in accord with the reforming spirit of the times, bishops have become less symbolic and more hardworking. He regrets the passing of the old panoply of wig and long apron and remoteness as valuable in that they help us venerate, and he has a sense that the act of veneration is psychologically beneficial to the venerator. But for the values we have lost, he says, we have a new honesty. The way to a bishopric used to be scholarship, or noble patronage, or pulpit eloquence in the presence of royalty, or skill in political pamphleteering; but now, and it has happened chiefly as a result of the self-examination and reform occasioned by the Oxford Movement, bishops are actually chosen for episcopal efficiency. It does happen that these efficient bishops have been Low Church men, but the efficiency is not necessarily connected to the Low-ness. "There are few, I think, now who remember much of the Low Church peculiarities of the Bishop of London, having forgotten all that in the results of his episcopate." This is presumably Blomfield, Bishop of London 1828–1856, very strongly a Sabbatarian, very strong against hunting parsons, very strong for fig-leaves on the nude statues at the Great Exhibition; a very hard-working man and great reformer, so practical that he was called the Right Reverend Utilitarian.

In actual fact, Melbourne when Prime Minister complained bitterly of the difficulties of appointing bishops. He said he was "continually subjected to the reproach of having disposed more ecclesiastical patronage than any other minister within so short a period, and of having so arranged it as neither to secure one steady personal friend, nor one firm supporter of my own principles" (Chadwick I, 123). Thirlwall was probably a mistake, being too learned and heterodox. Thomas Arnold never got it, being much too heterodox. Denison was very learned but was appointed nevertheless because he "never published books and was totally passive in theology." The witty Shuttleworth of New College nearly missed it because he was too worldly, "inventing a mahogany railway to carry decanters of port across the senior common room of his college". Melbourne "sighed wearily, and told Whately that he had had no notion of what a deal of trouble it was, reforming a church" (123-9).

Of course the reform is all to the good. Trollope points out there is still a conspicuous failure, an instance of that "sweet mediaeval flavour of Old English corruption". It is the bishops' own powers of patronage, still taken for granted. Trollope raises the interesting question, why should this practice remain longest in the Church? The Civil Service, the army and navy, and the legal profession have all "cleansed themselves". The Church might be expected to lead in matters of moral reform, rather than lag behind. One wonders, is it in truth because people feel the church matters less, or because they are reluctant to tamper with it? *Do* churches need to be more conservative than other institutions? As it was, the bishop in benefiting his friends "does not even know that he is doing amiss"! Trollope of course himself did the study of the classical case, not a bishop but a warden, Septimus Harding, the best of men and yet the beneficiary of an abuse. Mr Harding loses his innocence, and good man that he is rejects the benefice. Trollope's essay on bishops ends with the perfectly serious note that churchmen had better get "enlightened" on this matter, "by the voice of the laity whom they serve". One may consider that Trollope himself offers such enlightenment in his own novel *The Warden – prodesse aut delectare*.

III. *The Normal Dean of the Present Day*

The relationship of this fiction to a real life is best described by the actual response it drew from a real Dean, Henry Alford (see below). It could be noted here, though, that insofar as the Dean was responsible for the cathedral, his position seems to have been just as difficult as Trollope suggests. For as Chadwick writes, "Nearly all the Protestant countries dismantled their cathedrals during the Reformation, turned them into parish churches and used the endowment elsewhere . . . But the conservatism of the English Reformation preserved cathedrals and most of their funds." Finally the problem in the nineteenth century was that "No one knew what cathedrals were for" (I, 140–1). Alford may have resented Trollope coming so close to this conclusion, and may have thought he knew what cathedrals were for.

IV. *The Archdeacon*

Here there seems to be no need for annotation, and in fact to know Trollope's Archdeacon Grantly seems to be to know all there is to know about archdeacons. He is probably more real than any actual ones – very knowing as an administrator and man of business, knowing in politics, literature, wines and good living generally, and for all that probably a good man, too. The new "literate clergymen" Trollope refers to here as coming out of Islington and Birkenhead were a threat to the old Oxbridge gentleman style of Grantly;

these new schools trained men of the people for a new style clergyman, to purge the *gentleman-heresy* of the Church of England.

As for "Convocation", mentioned here: Anglican Convocations had been the merest vestigial formalities since 1717, but in 1852 the Convocation of Canterbury was reactivated, and that of York in 1861, to discuss if not to act on church business. One gathers from Trollope himself what its actual potency was then. In modern times it has become more important.

V. *The Parson of the Parish*

Here too Trollope maintains the gentleman-heresy, but grants that while the new style will win out, and is "less attractive, less urbane, less genial", it nevertheless may be more "energetic for God's word". This essay on the whole seems to me the most clear and classical, the most charitably witty; and as the parish parson is the very type of the English clergyman, so this essay is the most central and typical of these sketches. Novel readers will be pleased to recognise parsons like Trollope's Frank Fenwick, or George Eliot's Mr Irwine. Let not those who have read Trollope no farther than Barchester, however, believe that all Trollope's evangelicals are such as Obadiah Slope. There is a nice interplay in *The Claverings* (1867) between the hunting parson Henry Clavering – attractive, urbane, genial – who rather fails in clerical duty, and the evangelical curate Mr Saul who in his genuine devotion and integrity proves the better pastor. Clavering finally gives in with good grace, but in private, with his wife, he grieves a little: "Ah, I see how it is to be. There are to be no more cakes and ale in the parish." The echo of our classic English cry against the Puritans gives historical perspective to the incident.

VI. The Town Incumbent

Here there is considerable sociological interest, for we see a new kind of clergyman resulting from industrial change, part of the depersonalized society of the manufacturing town, and – as Trollope's comments on the word *incumbent* suggest – as poor in role and in tradition as the word itself when compared with *parson, vicar, rector*. Interesting questions of ecclesiastical economics are raised, and Trollope concludes with an argument rather parallel to the present arguments supporting the concept of tenure in academies. There is a strength in the Church of England, he says, that is due to the clergyman's independence from his popularity with his congregation. For the town incumbent is degraded to having his income depend on his preaching, and so, being a man like other men, is tempted to offer what sells. This puts him virtually in a lower social rank than his country confrère. What sells, in these days, are the smart questions of theology – doctrines and heresies and theories – rather than the ethical exhortation which Trollope feels is the proper office of the clergy-man and the need of the congregation. Thus the clergyman is compromised. But the skill to make a paying show out of disputations in theology is rare, it seems, and Trollope comes here to one of those some-what Johnsonian generalities about the quality of life: "he [the incumbent] probably fails. It is sad to say it, and sad to think of it, but failure is the ordinary lot of man."

As the clinching evidence that this position is too hard a test for poor humanity, Trollope has in the novels one noteworthy example, and this is the despicable Mr Emilius, a charlatan and a blackguard, who is involved with Lizzie in *The Eustace Diamonds* (1873) and not exposed until *Phineas Redux* (1874).

VII. *The College Fellow who has Taken Orders*

With this one I think we find Trollope somewhat out of his element. He did not know Oxford and Cam-bridge, and was inclined to feel a little sore about that ignorance. Hence the tone is rather mannered, the character never really emerges, and there is more criticism than character. The criticism seems valid enough – that there is no longer much logic in con-necting higher learning to the taking of orders, and Trollope arrives at at least one nice generality: "In the Church, because it is so picturesque and well-beloved in its old-fashioned garments, we can put up

with anomalies which elsewhere would be unendurable." Then we like to recognize Lazarus
College at Oxford, which we have heard of in Barchester as connected with Dr Gwynne and Mr
Arabin and Josiah Crawley; and the parish of Eiderdown which was, along with Crabtree Canonicorum
and Stogpingum, the cure of that resident-lepi-
dopterist of Lake Como in Italy, the Reverend Dr
Vesey Stanhope.

VIII. The Curate in a Populous Parish

This is perfectly eloquent and needs no more comment
than the questions Alford raised, and the answers, of
Josiah Crawley himself in *The Last Chronicle*, and of
the letter from "J. Altham" which proved Crawley
real (see below).

IX. The Irish Beneficed Clergyman

Ireland Trollope knew, and knew well. What better
field-work for a novelist than to begin as a Post
Office surveyor's clerk, then to be a surveyor, and
then to map and test rural delivery routes! This
explains Trollope's intimate knowledge of much of
England, but it was Ireland where he began the work,
in that part of his life when he first had a sense of his
own power and capacity. He "took on" Ireland with
great zest and curiosity, and his coming as an outsider

no doubt contributed to the acuity of his observation. This shows best in the sympathy and liveliness of his Irish novels, perhaps nowhere better than in the early and powerful *McDermots of Ballycloran* (1847).

At any rate, it is his understanding of Catholic Ireland that enables him to epitomize so graphically the representative of the minority religion there. This Protestant clergyman exists largely by his anti-Catholicism; "his clerical activities are always at work against enemies and not on behalf of friends", and this circumstance conditions all Protestant clergymen in Ireland, from bishops on down.

It is to be remembered that Trollope was writing at the time when it was generally granted that the Irish Church should be disestablished; reform had begun in 1833 with the Irish Church Bill that abolished two of the four Irish archbishoprics and eight of the bishoprics. Disestablishment did not come until 1871, however, and Trollope knew the urgency of the need for it. In these essays, it is at two points that the reformer's voice breaks through the gently satirical surface; first, on that matter of the grossly underpaid curates, and second, on the awful inequities in Ireland. His description of the tenor of these Anglicans in Ireland remains valid and illuminating. I myself, having many such among my own forbears, felt puzzled at their "fiery protestant zeal", the lack of the urbane grace I thought I could expect from Anglicans, and I never understood the situation until I read this essay of Trollope's.

X. The Clergyman who Subscribes for Colenso

In this last essay the Colenso case gives Trollope occasion for his most interesting essay on the nature of belief and how belief and orthodoxy can – and did – change. To review the case then, briefly:[12] Colenso himself had been a teacher of arithmetic, and carried over the literalist attitude into scriptural matters. He came to be Bishop of Natal, and did a translation of the Bible into Zulu. He loved and respected his Zulus, and respected their questions about the historical truth of the Old Testament, sought to test it arithmetically, and concluded that because the sums in the Pentateuch do not work out, the whole thing must be unhistorical. He was an oddly naïve man as well as warm-hearted and devout in spirit. He had read the famous *Essays and Reviews* (1860), by the "Seven Against Christ" as the orthodox literalists called them, distinguished scholars who applied the new learning in the German style to biblical texts, of whom the most famous were Mark Pattison and Benjamin Jowett. With much less learning, Colenso published his commentary on the Pentateuch. Like the authors of *Essays and Reviews*, but crudely, he called for a broadening of Anglican doctrine. *Essays and Reviews* was condemned in an encyclical in 1861, and condemned synodically in 1864. Colenso was in trouble, and the case posed a variety of dilemmas – administrative, legal, ecclesiastical and political, doctrinal, intellectual and moral. There were the predictable jokes about the bishop who went out to convert the heathen and came back converted by the heathen. There was a sort of excommunication and a sort of schism. Actually, Colenso returned to Natal in 1865 and functioned there as a churchman. Trollope himself heard him preach there in 1878. Meantime, Colenso's legal expenses were overwhelming, and scientists like Lyell and Darwin contributed to his relief fund. Trollope, with an eye ever alert for a test case, recognized how the fund afforded a sort of separation of the sheep from the goats – or the goats from the sheep, who was to say? So he envisages his broad-church clergyman obliged to go one way or the other, and finds he declares himself on the side of the new. The situation, like the central situations in his novels generally, is one of those interesting cases by which one discovers one's true interest, one's real moral bias, and in fact – or in action – defines the self.

It makes a good occasion to trace the subtle and gradual ways in which "beliefs" have changed. For his touchstone of the old days he refers to a fuss over that "certain professor of divinity at Oxford": this was the brouhaha of 1847 when Lord John Russell proposed R. D. Hampden for the see of Hereford, and the orthodox set up a roar. Hampden's breadth or liberalism seems to have consisted in a certain mildness toward Dissenters. *Mais nous avons changé tout cela*, explains Trollope. Now breadth even rejects miracles, and so on. One topical issue of the 'sixties and 'seventies that Trollope refers to was the "fulminating clause" of the Athanasian creed, that part of the *Quincunque Vult* which insists that he who does not keep the faith "shall perish everlastingly". However satisfying it may be to fulminate, the clause was bound to offend many in a humanitarian age. It became one of the cruxes of controversy, along with the question of how much we can remember the Sabbath day and keep it holy in an age of railways and progress.

What is most interesting in the essay is Trollope's version of an important Victorian – and post-Victorian – theme. Newman moves away from literalism and especially in his *Grammar of Assent* achieves a mode of argument that is psyche-centred rather than "truth"-centred. Pater would claim that religion consists in what we could call culture — ways of behaving, ways of feeling. Arnold inveighs against literalism, declares religion to be "three-fourths conduct", and proclaims the common ground of poetry and religion. Whatever that common ground is, it cannot be doctrine. All these great voices, that is, move the issue away from matters of true and false, and credal formulae. This essay is Trollope's own modest statement against literalism, along with his own note of nostalgia for the old certainties. It needs no more commentary. The virtue of it is that it is so clear. Just as it rejects the abstract in principle – Trollope is anti-systematic, anti-theoretic – it also rejects the abstract in practice, taking the novelist's way, to show us a human being.

THE ATTACK

These essays occasioned a little controversy – Trollope
writes in his *Autobiography* (167) that they were:

> considered to be of sufficient importance to bring
> down upon my head the critical wrath of a great
> dean of that period. The most ill-natured review
> that was ever written upon any work of mine
> appeared in the *Contemporary Review* with reference
> to these Clerical Sketches. The critic told me that I
> did not understand Greek. That charge has been
> made not infrequently by those who have felt
> themselves strong in that pride-producing language.
> It is much to read Greek with ease, but it is not
> disgraceful to be unable to do so. To pretend to
> read it without being able,—that is disgraceful. The
> critic, however, had been driven to wrath by my
> saying that Deans of the Church of England loved
> to revisit the glimpses of the metropolitan moon.

The "great dean", it was generally known, was
Henry Alford (1810–1871), Dean of Canterbury, a
voluminous scholar and writer. It is he to whom we
owe the 1839 edition of John Donne – *The Works* in
six volumes, with the "licentious" poems omitted.
(Alford does, however, wish "that the whole Poems
were well edited . . . but it seemed to me that the
character of this book being theological, The Poems
which were to be inserted should be of the same stamp"
[I, vii].) He was given to poetry himself, was one of
Tennyson's and Hallam's group at Cambridge,

published in 1832 his own *Poems and Poetical Fragments* which show some skill in the Wordsworthian style of meditative blank verse, wrote hymns both words and music (including "Come, ye thankful people, come!"), did a blank verse translation of the *Odyssey*; although evangelical in early training he later studied German and helped to make current the new ideas of German biblical scholarship, wrote a commentary on the Greek New Testament, was what we would call admirably tolerant of extremes within the Church, had some popularity as a lecturer on literary topics, edited *The Contemporary Review* and wrote a great deal for it, and for other periodicals. (See D.N.B. and a memoir by A. J. C. Hare in *Biographical Sketches* (1895)). He was a man of great energy, walked a lot – fast, and wrote a lot. His attack on Trollope shows his tendency to logorrhea. "Is it possible to write smartly on a matter of which one is almost entirely ignorant?" he begins, and the answer is yes, in twenty-two close-printed pages with no trace whatsoever of smartness or flippancy. ("Mr. Anthony Trollope and the English Clergy", *Contemporary Review* (June 1866), 240–62.) Three times Trollope is castigated for flippancy, and once even for "a want of earnestness".

Alford's main objection to Trollope's writings is its amateurism. Of course Trollope is being very deliberately the amateur; rather than giving us scholarship he describes what words like *chaplain*, *vicar*, etc. connote to the laity, thereby uncovering the images of the Church and its officers in men's minds. Alford feels obliged to correct and educate the public, to justify and defend the Church, and to tell his readers with precision a lot of things they will never remember. Probably Trollope should have checked his facts a little more, but Alford overdoes his attack. He reproves Trollope for his "extraordinary" idea that the medieval or Roman Catholic way of worship is for the glory of God, and the Protestant way is for the use of man. Quite properly as a theologian, Alford asserts the two things are really the same; but in truth Trollope's "extraordinary" idea is the merest commonplace, and he has characteristically guarded himself anyway with "it seems that", and "as we suppose". He is talking about the way these things are thought of, ever the psychological phenomenologist.

It would be perhaps a little hard for any Dean to have stomached Trollope on "The Normal Dean of the Present Day", and particularly hard for Alford. Trollope makes an analogy with architecture: in those old God-centred days churches had adornments "which no mortal eye can reach", suggesting that deans are now adornments of no mortal use. In comparison with bishops, say, they are quite supernumerary: "the change from a deanery . . . to a palace is a change from ease to work, from leisure to turmoil". The dean's income is less than a bishop's, but his expenses very much less, and so he is "sleek" – this did rile Alford. It is not Trollope's wittiest barb, and certainly below any dignified dean's notice, and Alford should not have risen to it. "It is the *snob-*

bishness of it which we are challenging, rather than its want of truth"; but he impugns that too. Such defence is pure loss. When Trollope writes that the chief qualification for a deanery is a taste for literature, the bellettrist side of Alford is much offended: a dean's taking of orders, Trollope suggests, is only an accident of circumstances; being scholars, deans are too liberal in their views to be appointed bishops; if the government had kept Colenso a dean in England, there would have been no trouble. Of course, all this would be deeply galling to the scholarly, 'liberal' Alford whose piety and vocation seem to be perfectly genuine anyway. Trollope's diagnosis of the reasons behind Alford's attack is probably quite accurate.

Alford attacks on all flanks, however; he goes on about curates' incomes at great length – a strategic mistake, it will turn out; he catches Trollope in error on the College Fellow, an error so awful that *"Even the American* [my italics] Mr. Everett might have saved him from it" (that Fellows were originally instituted as monks); on the subject of bishops, Alford moves in on Trollope's grammar – his use of prepositions evidences a most culpable ignorance of Greek etymologies; and he is entirely wrong, says Alford, on the Irish churchman, even though even a modern reader can recognize Trollope's truth. Alford is so moved by his own arguments, however, that he declares "The production of such a book as this cannot be looked on as other than a serious public evil." He says journalism in general these days is deplorably frivolous about ecclesiastical matters; even *The Times* is guilty, and it is too bad that instead of writing properly, "our best writers . . . indite Theophrastic caricatures of the clergy."

How to write properly about the Church? Alford gives – at length – some samples, by describing his own reform ideas: one, that there be more lay helpers for the clergy, and two, that we stamp out the deplorable cheap ready-made sermon-services that some of the clergy subscribe to. He quotes with horror two and a half pages of advertisements for ready-made sermons, culled from the professional journals: ". . . Utmost Satisfaction . . . Strictest Confidence . . .," etc. – all this to our delight in these irreverent latter days. Then, oddly enough, Alford returns to Trollope with a changed tune. He wants to "part friends" and finds he can "almost unreservedly praise" the last essay, "The Clergyman who Subscribes for Colenso". "It is a piece of capital description, not overdone." He gets in another dig, though: "The writer is evidently more at home among the phenomena of unbelief, than among those of undoubting faith and obedience." Finally it would seem that Alford does indeed appreciate the sympathy and perspicuity of that interesting last essay, and he might have looked rather good to posterity if he had had less easy access to print.

There was another clerical attack on Trollope in another clerical journal, *The Guardian* (6 June 1866, 602), which like Alford's specifically denied that curates still received stipends of so little as Trollope claimed, £70 per annum. Immediately after Trollope wrote these essays he proceeded to the writing of *The Last Chronicle of Barset*, with its memorable story of a case in point, poor Josiah Crawley, perpetual curate at Hogglestock. Suddenly the voice of a real-life Josiah Crawley materializes in the pages of *The Guardian* itself (18 July, 748):

Sir—In your notice (June 6) of the above-mentioned book you say, "It is unworthy of Mr. Trollope to endorse a popular error in such a sentence as the following:—'It is notorious that a rector of the Church of England, in possession of a living of, let us say a thousand a year, shall employ a curate at seventy pounds a year, that the curate shall do three-fourths or more of the work of the parish, that he shall remain in that position for twenty years, taking one-fourteenth of the wages while he does three-fourths of the work, and that nobody shall think that the rector is wrong or the curate ill-used!'"
"Such a picture," you proceed to say, "was common in novels of the last generation, but we doubt whether it was even then often found in reality, and we are tolerably certain that Mr. Trollope would have to hunt very diligently before he could unearth such a case at present. He would probably say in answer, that his sketches partake of the nature of caricature, and require a little exaggeration of the more grotesque features to make them telling; and, with this understanding, we may

afford to laugh over them." In reply to these observations of yours, I wish to say that I can produce such a case (and during my life have known many more such cases) as Mr. Trollope so graphically describes. It is my own. I have laboured hard as a curate, &c., for the last forty years, sometimes in very populous parishes, and at small stipends, and on benefices of large income, without any material advance in remuneration. For some years I served a curacy, the living of which was very nearly £1,000 a year, with a stipend of £75; and on another occasion, with a stipend of £100, on a benefice of beyond £900 a year. Another cure I served nearly twelve years on a stipend of £70, and yet was never offered anything better, nor my case considered a hard one. J. Altham.

Holmpton, June 25, 1866.

History too confirms Trollope's accuracy: Owen Chadwick records that in "the Exeter diocese of 1866 sixty-eight clergymen remained assistant curates on an average income of £100, though all had served at least fifteen years, and sometimes up to fifty years" (I, 158). The *Pall Mall* moved quickly to say (20 July 1866, 9) that "as Mr. Trollope's statement appeared in our own columns, we ought to be pleased at this confirmation of his accuracy", but went on to say that of course it is sad evidence of continuing need for reform. Then Trollope himself, in the issue of July 24, 3–4, adds his own plea:

Sir,—In your impression for last Friday there is a short notice referring to the incomes of curates, in which allusion is made to the "rough handling" given by certain Church periodicals to my little volume on Clergymen of the Church of England. I care little for the rough handling as personal to myself, if only it may be the means of drawing continued attention to that special subject which has brought down upon me the worst of the flagellation,—namely the salaries now paid to curates for their work; and I was especially glad to see your notice on the subject the other day, because it contained a strong corroboration from an old curate, who had acted in one richly endowed parish after another, of the statements I had made and of the opinions I had expressed.

I have been especially "roughly handled" because I named £70 per annum as the normal income of a curate. And in one such very rough handling I was grievously punished by, I presume, a clerical gentleman (probably not a curate), who published a list of the incomes allotted by law to curates, showing that those incomes are by law proportioned to the population of the parishes in which the curate is called upon to act;—that the lowest sum so sanctioned by law is £80 per annum, and that the highest actually rises to the liberal remuneration of £150 per annum, for the full occupation of a clergyman's time! As I had named £70 per annum as the normal allowance for a curate, and as the minimum of £80 is £10 in excess of my "normal" salary, this would have been disagreeable to me, had not the writer of the article, in giving his list of salaries, felt himself constrained to state that these salaries had no reference whatever to that class of curates with whom I had manifestly been dealing. I had spoken of ordinary curates,—the "normal" curates,—the every-day curates, with whom and with whose state any member of the Church of England is acquainted, —whose work is done under a vicar or rector, and in connection with that superior parochial clergyman, whereas the list sanctioned by law refers only to curates who are called upon to act in parishes without any other resident clergyman. These liberal incomes therefore of £150, £135, and £120 per annum have no bearing whatever on the question as raised by me in my reference to the normal £70; but yet to the ordinary reader, the list would seem to be an answer. A statement of the incomes of the bishops could not have been a less apposite answer.

But I should not trouble you with all this now,— knowing well that these little differences between authors and critics, and between critics and counter-critics are not interesting to the public,—were it not that something may perhaps be gained by a reference to such admissions as have been made by those who assert that the payments given to curates are sufficient. I still maintain that £70 in hard cash is, throughout the rural parishes of

England, the salary at which a rector or a vicar thinks that he ought to get a curate. There is nothing in the law to prevent his getting one for £50 if he can. My opponents say that these salaries range up from even £80 to £100, to almost any amount,—even to £150! My supporter, to whom your note refers, though he served for twelve years on what I have called the normal salary of £70, nevertheless did, during certain other years, earn £75, and seems to have culminated in one period at £100. Suppose, for the sake of the argument, that we drop the £70, and,—in the teeth of evidence to the contrary,—speak of the income of curates as vacillating between £80 and £150, the incomes paid by law for curates where there are no resident incumbents. What in such cases as that shall we say of the incomes of our clerical labourers? In these days, in which the need for clergymen has increased so very much quicker than endowments have increased or can be made to increase, men who go into the Church without interest must remain there as curates for ten years,—for twenty years,— for life. Is there any profession in which such salaries will obtain the services of efficient men in the prime of life? Is there any other profession in which efficient men in the prime of life cannot obtain a much more adequate payment for their work? Both these questions must be answered in the negative. No man will say that even £150 per annum will properly support a clergyman of the age of forty;—

or will say that any educated gentleman will consider himself to be properly paid for his work by £150 per annum.

The members of the Church of England, however, are as willing to pay their clergymen as they are to pay their doctors or their lawyers. But the present nature of the Church Establishment, as an endowed Church,—as a Church in possession of a fixed property supposed to be sufficient to support itself, —is altogether antagonistic to that increase in the total amount of remuneration required which the increase in population demands. That the idea of an endowment should be very pleasant to a learned dean, revisiting, as I ventured before profanely to remark, the glimpses of the metropolitan moon, and looking with well-pleased eyes on the pleasant things around him, is natural enough. But to the people who want the services of a clergyman, a married curate,—or a married incumbent of a district,— with £150 per annum for all his wants, is not a pleasant sight either in a religious, or in a social, or in a professional point of view. The country can afford to pay him better for his work, and would do so if things were placed on a better footing.

Anthony Trollope

The whole little episode is a rather interesting instance of the relationship of gentle satire to history.

NOTES

1 Published as separate essays in *Punch*, 1846–7; collected in *The Book of Snobs* (1848).

2 See Bradford A. Booth, 'Trollope and the "Pall Mall"', *Nineteenth-Century Fiction*, IV (June and September 1949), 51–69, 137–158.

3 Volumes I and II (1970–1). These are volumes VII and VIII of *An Ecclesiastical History of England*. Ensuing references are to *The Victorian Church*, volumes I and II.

4 *Autobiography*, ed. Bradford A. Booth (1947), 185.

5 *Letters*, ed. Gordon S. Haight, IV (1954), 81–2.

6 *Trollope, Artist and Moralist* (London, 1971), published concurrently as *The Moral Trollope* (Ohio).

7 *Thackeray*, English Men of Letters Series (1897), 203–5.

8 *The Complete Prose Works of Matthew Arnold*, ed. R. H. Super (Michigan, 1972), vol. III, 80.

9 See, for example, *Prose*, VIII, 135.

10 Anthony Trollope, *Cicero* (2 vols, 1880), II, 352.

11 *The Victorian Church in Decline* (1969), 6.

12 See Chadwick II, 90–7, and A. O. J. Cockshut, *Anglican Attitudes* (1959), 88 ff.

APPENDIX

Introductory Note

Anthony Trollope, 'The Zulu in London', *Pall Mall Gazette* (10 May 1865), 3–4.

The editor of the *Pall Mall Gazette* had asked Trollope to do a series of reports on the 'May meetings' at Exeter Hall; these were assemblies of Evangelicals whose type of religion had come to be called the 'Exeter Hall' kind of thing. As Trollope tells in his *Autobiography* (169) he went to one, and wrote one report, but that was all he could stand, and he begged off the rest. The report he did do, however, though it is slight (and commits a terribly desperate pun – *canon-cannon*), is of some interest. First, for Trollope's art: he turns characteristically to the literary device of the foreign observer, to reveal our non-foreign selves to us in a fresh light. Compare the technique of his novel *The American Senator* (1877), and his peculiar Carlylean satire *The New Zealander* (ed. N. John Hall, 1972). Second, because the foreign observer here is one of Colenso's Zulu friends, we get in this sketch some amusingly ironic criticism of the Evangelicals' attitude to the Colenso case. Finally, there is a feminist touch: Trollope seems to be defending the rights of English women to their share of religious doubt, along with men.

THE ZULU IN LONDON.

To the EDITOR *of the* PALL MALL GAZETTE.

SIR,—Favourable circumstances having enabled me to visit the great centre of the Christian religion, my wishes and my duty carried me to one of your May meetings at the Hall of Exeter as the first object of my eager curiosity. I had hoped to have enjoyed the privilege of attending this meeting, which was devoted to the propagation of Christianity among the Jews, in the company of a well-known bishop of the Christian Church, with whom I had enjoyed closely intimate connections in my own country a few years since; but it was explained to me, on his behalf, that, zealous as is that excellent pastor in the cause of religion, his zeal is not of the sort which is palatable to the customary worshippers in the Hall of Exeter. And when I urged the matter, explaining that a Christian bishop should not be afraid of facing any Christian people, the friend of my friend went on to assure me with much energy that he whom I had known at home as an ardent missionary in the cause of Christianity, would be torn limb from limb within the Hall, should he venture to show himself among the crowd of brother missionaries which was about to be there assembled. To understand this was at first to me an impossibility, for I had been told that toleration was the grand characteristic of the English Protestant Church. But by degrees I have come to perceive that the pastor and bishop of the people to whom I belong is supposed to have been a traitor to his own religion, to have fouled his own nest (as a worthy gentleman with a warm red face and a white neckcloth said to me at the meeting); and that the English QUEEN, and the English Parliament, and the English hierarchy have all set their faces against him; but in vain, as with all their united efforts they cannot make him to cease from being a bishop among them. And when I remembered, Mr. Editor, that I myself— even I—had, under Providence, been the humble instrument of teaching to my worthy friend some of those proved facts in reference to the old Mosaic scriptures which are now quite recognized among Christians in my own country, but which seem to be so unpalatable here, and began to reflect that I had been the primary cause of all the trouble which this good man is made to endure, my heart trembled within me, and I almost feared to face this mutiny of your infuriated English Christians. "What will they do to the Zulu," I asked, "if such be their treatment of the Zulu's friend and pupil?" For my heart swelled within me as I remembered certain passages in our religious conferences at home, wherein the bishop had learned, perhaps, more than he had taught. But my companion reassured me, giving me to understand that if I would put on a black coat and black gloves, and tie a white cravat round my neck, my Zulu relationship would not be suspected; and when I conformed myself to his advice, he complimented my appearance by declaring that the customary worshippers in the Hall of Exeter would take me for a converted Jew. But, as you will hear, Sir, there came a time during the meeting at which I was sure that one energetic gentleman there knew well who I was, and I must confess that my fear nearly overcame me, till zeal in my cause overcame even my fears.

What a magnificent chamber is that Hall of Exeter – though, indeed, the stairs by which I was taken up to my seat were of the narrowest. I was so far honoured as to be put on the platform; but I found that unless I were a lady that honour was a matter of course. All the gentlemen, about a hundred and fifty in number, were on the platform, whereas the ladies below were there in thousands. Whether they were pretty I could not see, but they were very industrious, having needle and thread at hand, and working diligently through many of the discourses. We who make sermons at home would not like this treatment, thinking that our women's minds are not big enough for two employments at once; but here, in England, perhaps they are bigger. Yes; I was on the platform and sat nearly behind a big chair, in which there was, as I was told, a noble lord whose constant employment it is to sit in that chair. I wish I could have seen the face of the noble lord, but I saw only the back of his head. But he, though he sat in the big chair, really took no part in the meeting except to tell us the names of those who were going to preach; and if such really be his daily work I hope that he finds some compensation in its easiness for the weariness which it must certainly create. At first we had prayers and then a hymn—which they told me was sung by converted Jew children. I was close to them, and thought they looked like Christians from the birth; but at any rate they sang the hymn well, and as I heard the sounds swelling through the vault of that glorious room, I rejoiced in my soul that I had come to your country— forgetting for a while those Christian feuds of which I had heard. Ah! if it could all be like that hymn!

After the hymn a stout gentleman read a long paper about the Jews; but, though I was near to him, I could not hear a word. A few figures I did catch, which told me that his report dealt only with tens and twenties, whereas among us our dealings are with hundreds and thousands. But the Jews are a stubborn people, and from such the evil spirit does not come out without many struggles. At first I grieved much that I did not hear, but after a while I perceived that this was the part of the morning's work which excited the least interest. It was not to hear how many Jewish children had been baptized that all those ladies had brought thither their sewing. While the stout gentleman read from his paper they sewed diligently, and I could perceive that a clergyman to the right of me and a clergyman to the left yawned painfully. But it was when the stout gentleman had done that the interest of the day commenced. The lord in the chair then told us that a certain right rev. prelate would say a few words, and a very nice-looking gentleman got up on the lord's right hand, whom I would not have guessed to be a bishop by any outward sign—seeing him, as it was my chance to do, from behind—and said more than a few words. But he was so eloquent, that methought he said not a word too many. It was true that he said little or nothing about the Jews, but dilated greatly on the benefit done by missionary work in general, and on the blessings which had been disseminated throughout the world by that evangelical party in the Church to which he belonged. I am sure that that bishop is a good man, and I wished that I might have been able to talk to him as it was my privilege to do a few years since with our own bishop at home. Doubtless, in that case, I should learn much; but, perhaps, I might be enabled to teach something also. As the bishop delivered his sermon I perceived that the sewing became slack among the ladies, and I saw that they possessed no special power of using their fingers and their ears together.

The bishop, however, eloquent though he was, and applauded with many cheers, was not the star of the occasion. After the bishop there arose a gentleman, who, as it seemed, did say something of the Jews, only I could not hear a word, and I observed that while he spoke the needles and threads were going vigorously. But when this gentleman sat down, then I could perceive from the very manner in which the noble lord moved his head that the real thing was coming, and that the excitement of the day was at hand. On the left of the noble lord sat a gentleman whose beautiful silver-white hair had already attracted much of my attention, and who was now summoned to his feet. He was called a canon—somewhat, I suppose, as LUTHER has been called the great Protestant bomb—and he appeared well worthy of his name. When he turned to us on the platform, as he did frequently—too frequently indeed for me, as I shall have to explain to you—I perceived that he was a handsome man, by no means old as his silver locks had seemed to show, but still possessing all the vigour of manhood, and with it much of grace and eloquence. When he arose, not a needle moved again till he had finished. But, Sir, this canon did not say a word about the Jews till he had reached the end of his discourse, and then only a word or two of no import, as instigated by the necessity of the occasion.

What was my surprise, Mr. Editor, you may guess, when I found that throughout his address he was talking almost entirely of me. Of me—that is, as far as it had been my privilege to open the eyes of our bishop at home to the physical impossibility of certain occurrences related in the Old Testament. And when the rev. canon turned round, looking me full in the face, as he did repeatedly, I could not but think that he knew me as a hostile Zulu in spite of my white cravat, and that he was intending to demolish me personally. The kind friend who had been deputed by our bishop to accompany me to the meeting was good enough to assure me frequently that this could not be the case, and that the canon had prepared every word that he was uttering before he could have known of my intended presence; but, if so, why did he confine himself to an attack upon my views of the Old Testament at a meeting held for the conversion of the Jews! On that head there could be nothing that he would wish to change in the belief of any Jew.

The canon, though beautiful to the eyes, and eloquent beyond measure, and very energetic, was so unjust in his arguments that thrice I attempted to rise on my legs in order that I might confute him by a word; but my friend held me down by those odious coat-tails which I had assumed, and would not let me speak. He told me that no discussion was allowed in the Hall of Exeter, and that the audience there assembled would listen to no arguments opposed to their own established modes of believing. If this be so, of what use is the Hall of Exeter? Who will be served if nobody therein may be converted from any error to any truth? If all be right with them already, why should they go there at all? And if there be aught wanting to them, why not let them listen to debate? Therefore, Sir, I rush to you to cry out against that canon's false logic and erroneous teaching.

And what was his teaching? It can be told in a word. Our SAVIOUR had said that the Scriptures cannot be

broken, and therefore, declared the canon, every word
in the Old Testament, as translated into English, must
be true. The moon did stand still, and by inference the
sun did ordinarily, in the days of JOSHUA, move round
the earth, seeing that it is declared to have stood still
miraculously upon one special occasion only. But the
canon went into none of these little difficulties,
though he dilated on his own view of the case for
nearly an hour. Our SAVIOUR had said that the
Scriptures cannot be broken,—meaning, doubtless,
that the law, as written in the Old Testament, was to
be held as binding in all its statutes,—and this one
word sufficed for the canon as a full answer to all those
distressing questions which have lately been trans-
ferred from the African Church to your Church here
in England! How easy a thing must faith be to him if
he can satisfy his doubts after such a fashion as this!
Would it not have been better that the canon should
have confined himself to the Jews, and have left me
and my doubts,—doubts, Mr. Editor, which harass
my soul,—to be questioned and, if possible, set at
rest by some more astute debater.

And then there came from him words which made
me think that I could not be among a Protestant
people, or whether I had not rather strayed into some
Mahomedan congregation in which the weakness of
the woman is held in contempt by the strength and
wisdom of man. For the canon, turning his back upon
the ladies, with his face towards the clergy on the
platform, and with his eyes, as I thought, firmly

fixed upon myself, implored us to keep any doubts we might have to ourselves; "and do not", said he, "do not, I implore you, vex with such reasonings the "minds of these poor ignorant ones whom it is your "duty to guide in the right way". Then he waved his white hand gracefully over the heads of the ladies, and again as he did so repeated his prayer—"Let not these poor ignorant ones be vexed with vain doubts." Now, Mr. Editor, let me tell you that Zulu women would not stand such a treatment as that. In what we believe and what we don't believe our women go along with us; and men and women both among us will receive nothing into their faith which is too gross for the belief of their teachers. In my own land histories have come to us, telling us that among an ancient people that had many priests, the people believed, but the priests believed nothing. It was held that it was a good thing to restrain the minds of the populace by a religion which was known to be a farce by those who administered its ceremonies. I have heard, too, suspicion expressed that something of the same hypocrisy had crept into the priesthood of the older branch of our great Christian Church, though as to that I say nothing of my own knowledge. But I certainly had not expected to hear such a mode of teaching boldly advocated in the Hall of Exeter!

That reverend prelate who had before spoken had told us that controversy is better than unreasoning tranquillity in religion, as a rushing torrent is better than a stagnant pool. I honoured him as he spoke those words, and longed to hurl them at the canon's head when he talked of the poor ignorant flocks from whom the clergy should keep all doubtful questions. But no one save myself seemed to feel any indignation, and when the canon sat down, the "ignorant" ladies to whom he had thus pointed cheered him to the echo. For myself I simply resolved that I would not pass another morning within the Hall of Exeter during my sojourn in this city.—Your faithful friend,

A ZULU IN LONDON.

BIBLIOGRAPHICAL NOTE

Clergymen of the Church of England was first published in serial form in volumes II and III of *The Pall Mall Gazette: An Evening Newspaper and Review*. The ten parts appeared on the following dates:

Monday 20 November 1865
Monday 27 November 1865
Saturday 2 December 1865
Monday 11 December 1865
Monday 18 December 1865
Friday 29 December 1865
Friday 5 January 1866
Saturday 20 January 1866
Tuesday 23 January 1866
Thursday 25 January 1866

All parts were published anonymously.

In 1866 the work was issued as a volume: *Clergymen of the Church of England. By Anthony Trollope. [Reprinted from the "Pall Mall Gazette."]* This edition was published in London by Chapman and Hall. The ten chapters of the book correspond to the parts as originally published in the *Pall Mall Gazette*. The type was reset for this edition and several minor textual alterations were made. More significantly, there were also a few additions, notably in chapter VIII on pages 96–9 of the book text. These have the effect of strengthening Trollope's argument about the injustices of the curate's position. In chapter I the final sentence on page 7 is an addition.

In his bibliographical description of the novel in *Trollope: A Bibliography* (London, Constable, 1928) Michael Sadleir gives the date of publication of the volume as 30 March 1866. He notes slight variants in three individual copies of the book and also finds that the volume was originally intended to appear with the title *Clerical Sketches*.

The present volume reprints photographically the text of the 1866 volume. No subsequent editions of the work have been published.

J. L. Madden

CLERGYMEN

OF THE

CHURCH OF ENGLAND.

BY

ANTHONY TROLLOPE.

[REPRINTED FROM THE "PALL MALL GAZETTE."]

LONDON:

CHAPMAN AND HALL, 193, PICCADILLY.

1866.

CONTENTS.

——◆◇◆——

CLERGYMEN

CHURCH OF ENGLAND.

I.

THE MODERN ENGLISH ARCHBISHOP.

THE old English archbishop was always a prince in
the old times, but the English archbishop is a prince
no longer in these latter days. He is still a nobleman
of the highest rank,—he of Canterbury holding his
degree, indeed, above all his peers in Parliament, not
of Royal blood, and he of York following his elder
brother, with none between them but the temporary
occupant of the woolsack. He is still one before
whose greatness small clerical aspirants veil their
eyes, and whose blessing in the minds of pious
maidens has in it something almost divine. He is,

as I have said, a peer of Parliament. Above all things, he should be a gentleman, and,—if it were always possible,—a gentleman of birth ; but he has no longer anything of the position or of the attributes of a prince.

And this change has come upon our archbishops quite in latter times; though, of course, we must look back to the old days of Papal supremacy in England for the prince archbishop of the highest class. Such careers as those of Thomas à Becket or of Wolsey have not been possible to any clergymen since the days in which the power of the Pope was held to be higher on matters ecclesiastical than the power of the Crown in these realms; but we have had among us prince archbishops to a very late date,— archbishops who have been princes not by means of political strength or even by the force of sacerdotal independence, but who have enjoyed their principalities simply as the results of their high rank, their wealth, their reserve, their inaccessibility, as the result of a certain mystery as to the nature of their duties,—and sometimes as the result of personal veneration. For this personal veneration personal dignity was as much needed as piety, and was much more necessary than high mental power. An archbishop of fifty years since was very difficult to approach, but when approached was as urbane as a king,—who is supposed never to be severe but at a distance. He lived almost royally, and his palace received that respect which seems, from the nature of the word, to be due to a palatial residence. What he did, no man but his own right-hand chaplain knew with accuracy; but that he could shower church patronage as from the east the west and the south, all clerical aspirants felt,—with awe rather than with hope. Lambeth in those days was not overshadowed by the opposite glories of Westminster. He of York, too, was a Northern prince, whose hospitalities north of the Humber were more in repute than those of earls and barons. Fifty years since the archbishops were indeed princes; but now-a-days we have changed all that. The change, however, is only now completed. It was but the other day that there died an Archbishop of Armagh who was prince to the backbone, princely in his wealth and princely in his use of it, princely in his mode of life, princely in his gait and outer looks and personal demeanour,— princely also in the performance of his work. He made no speeches from platforms. He wrote no books. He was never common among men. He was a fine old man ; and we may say of him that he was the last of the prince archbishops.

This change has been brought about, partly by the altered position of men in reference to each other, partly also by the altered circumstances of the arch- bishops themselves. We in our English life are daily approaching nearer to that republican level which is equally averse to high summits and to low depths. We no longer wish to have princes among us, and will at any rate have none of that mysterious kind which is half divine and half hocus- pocus. Such terrestrial gods as we worship we choose to look full in the face. We must hear their voices and be satisfied that they have approved themselves as gods by other wisdom than that which lies in the wig. That there is a tendency to evil in this as well as a tendency to good may be true enough. To be able to venerate is a high quality, and it is coming to that with us, that we do not now venerate much. In this way the altered minds of men have altered the position of the archbishops of the Church of England.

But the altered circumstances of the sees themselves have perhaps done as much as the altered tendencies of men's minds. It is not simply that the incomes received by the present archbishops are much less than the incomes of their predecessors,—though that alone would have done much,—but the incomes are of a nature much less prone to produce princes. The territorial grandeur is gone. The archbishops and bishops of to-day, with the exception of, I believe, but two veterans on the bench, receive their allotted stipends as do the clerks in the Custom-house. There is no longer left with them any vestige of the power of the freehold magnate over the soil. They no longer have tenant and audit days. They cannot run their lives against leases, take up fines on renewals, stretch their arms as possessors over wide fields, or cut down woods and put acres of oaks into their ecclesiastical pockets. They who understand the nature of the life of our English magnates, whether noble or not noble, will be aware of the worth of that territorial position of which our bishops have been deprived under the working of the Ecclesiastical Commission. The very loss of the risk has been much!—as that man looms larger to himself, and therefore to others also, whose receipts may range from two to six hundred a year, than does the comfortable possessor of the insured medium. The actual diminution of income, too, has done much, and this has been accompanied by so great a rise in the price of all princely luxuries that an archbishop without a vast private fortune can no longer live as princes should live. In these days, when a plain footman demands his fifty pounds of yearly wages, and three hundred pounds a year is but a moderate rent for a London house, an archbishop cannot support a semi-royal retinue or live with much palatial splendour in the metropolis upon an annual income of eight thousand pounds.

And then, above all, the archbishops have laid aside their wigs.

That we shall never have another prince archbishop in England or in Ireland may be taken to be almost certain. Whether or no we shall ever have prelates at Canterbury or York, at Armagh or Dublin, gifted with the virtues and vices of princely minds, endowed with the strength and at the same time with the self-willed obstinacy of princes, may be doubtful. There is scope enough for such strength and such obstinacy in the position, and our deficiency or our security,—as each of us according to his own idiosyncrasy may regard it,—must depend, as it has latterly been caused, by the selections made by the Prime Minister of the day. There is the scope for strength and obstinacy now almost as fully as there was in the days of Thomas à Becket, though the effects of such strength or obstinacy would of course be much less wide. And, indeed, as an archbishop may be supposed in these days to be secure from murder, his scope may be said to be the fuller. What may not an archbishop say, and what may not an archbishop do, and that without fear of the only punishment which could possibly reach an archbishop,—the punishment, namely, of deprivation? With what caution must not a Minister of the present day be armed to save him from the misfortune of having placed an archbishop militant over the Church of England?

The independence of an archbishop, and indeed to a very great, though lesser extent of a bishop, in the midst of the existing dependence of all others around him, would be a singular phenomenon, were it not the natural result of our English abhorrence of change. We hate an evil, and we hate a change. Hating the evil most, we make the change, but we make it as small as possible. Hence it is that our Archbishop of Canterbury has so much of that independent power which made Thomas à Becket fly against his sovereign when the archiepiscopal mitre was placed upon his head, though he had been that sovereign's most obedient servant till his consecration. Thomas à Becket held his office independently of the king; and so does Dr. Longley. The Queen, though she be the head of the Church, cannot rid herself of an archbishop who displeases her. The Queen, in speaking of whom in our present sense of course we mean the Prime Minister, can make an Archbishop of Canterbury; but she cannot unmake him. The archbishop would be safe, let him play what tricks he might in his high office. Nothing short of a commission de lunatico inquirendo could attack

him successfully,—which, should it find his grace to
be insane, would leave him his temporalities and his
titles, and simply place his duties in the hands of a
coadjutor.   Should an archbishop commit a murder,
or bigamy, or pick a pocket, he, no doubt, would be
liable to the laws of his country; but no lawyer and
no statesman can say to what penalties he can be
subjected as regards the due performance of the
duties of his office.   A judge is independent;—that
is, he is not subject to any penalty in regard to any
exercise of his judicial authority; but we all know
that a judge would soon cease to be a judge who
should play pranks upon the bench, or decline to
perform the duties of his position.   The archbishops,
as the heads of the endowed clergymen of the Church
of England, are possessed of freeholds, and that freehold cannot be touched.   It is theirs for life; and so
great is the practical latitude of our Church, that it
may be doubted whether anything short of a professed
obedience to the Pope could deprive an archbishop of
his stipend.

It may, therefore, be easily understood that a
Prime Minister, in selecting an archbishop, has a

difficult task in hand. He is bound to appoint a man who not only has hitherto played no pranks, but of whom he may feel sure that he will play none in future. In our Church, as it exists at present, we have ample latitude joined to much bigotry, and it is almost as impossible to control the one as the other. Such control is, in fact, on either side absolutely impossible; and, therefore, archbishops are wanted who shall make no attempts at controlling. And yet an archbishop must seem to control,—or, else, why is he there? An Archbishop of Canterbury must be a visible head of bishops, and yet exercise no headship. He must appear to men as the great guide of parsons, but his guidance must not go beyond advice, and of that the more chary he may be, the better will be the archbishop. Of course it will be understood that reference is here made to doctrinal guidance, and not to moral guidance—to latitude or bigotry in matters of religion, and not to the social conduct of clergymen. How difficult then must be the position of a Minister who has to select for so dangerous a place a clergyman who shall be great enough to fill it, and yet small enough; and one who shall also be just enough to remember always that he is bound to retain that quiescence for which credit was given him when he was chosen? The archbishop must be a man without any latent flame, without ambition, desirous of no noise, who shall be content to have been an archbishop without leaving behind him a peculiar name among his brethren. He should hope to be remembered only as a good old man, who in troublesome times abated some trouble and caused none, who smiled often and frowned but seldom, who wore his ecclesiastical robes on high days with a grace, and exercised a modest and frequent hospitality, having no undue desire to amass money for his children.

It is not, perhaps, too much to say that the sort of man exactly wanted may be selected for any post, and be found adequate to the required duties so long as the sword of deprivation or dismissal can be made to hang over the occupant's head. But it is very difficult to find a man who shall do his work, not after the fashion which may seem best to himself, but in the way which seems most desirable to others, who, when once placed, cannot be removed from his

place. Will your groom or your gardener obey you
with that precision which you desire when he comes
to know that you cannot rid yourself of his services?
And human nature is the same in gardeners and
in archbishops. It is not that the man is void of
conscience and that he resolves to disobey where he
has promised to obey, but that he tells himself that
in his position duty requires no obedience. Your
gardener with a taste for tulips would, under such
circumstances, grow nothing but tulips; and what is
to hinder your archbishop from putting down the
miracles or putting up candlesticks? With Lambeth
all ablaze with candlesticks the archbishop would still
hold his place.

The same thing may be said of the bishops; but
among so many bishops it is felt to be well that there
should be some few who shall have a flame of their
own. In the house that has many rooms the owner
may indulge in many colours on the walls, and some
of them may be of the brightest; but in the house
that has but one or two chambers the colours should
be chosen with a due regard to the ordinary quiescence
of every-day life. Had we not High Church and Low

Church among our ordinary bishops, were we to be deprived of our dear —— and our dear ——, we should miss much that we feel to be ornamental to the Establishment and useful to ourselves. There are a few among us of course who would be glad to see lights of the same splendour, even though so dangerous, at Canterbury and at York; but it behoves a Prime Minister to be a moderate man, and a man moderate, above all things, in religion. In the religion of to-day moderation is everything. And, therefore, whatever else he may be, let the archbishop be a moderate man. Let him always be throwing oil upon waters. Nothing should shock him—nothing, that is, in the way of religion. Nothing should excite him ; nothing should make him angry. He should be a man able to preach well, but not inclined to preach often. In his preaching he should charm the ears of all hearers, but he should hardly venture to stir their pulses. He should speak, too, occasionally from platforms and chairs ; only let him not make himself too common. He should be very affable on Mondays and Tuesdays, secluding himself somewhat on the other five days of the week, answering his correspondents with words which may mean as little as words can be made to mean, and carefully watching that he commits himself to nothing. How hard it is to find the man who shall have talent enough for this, and yet the self-command never to go beyond it, even though no penalties await him, except such as may come from the venomous baiting of other clergymen.

But it must not be supposed that the archbishop of to-day can be, or should be, an idle man. It is his duty to be the precursor—probably the unconscious precursor—of other men in that religion which shall teach us that the ways of God are very easy to find, though they may not be so easy to follow; that forms are almost nothing, so that faith be there. Of all men, an archbishop should be the least of a fanatic. Can any one imagine an archbishop of the present day abhorring a Dissenter, or refusing to dine with a Roman Catholic because of his religion ? And to do this is much, even though it be done unconsciously. An archbishop thus leading the van against bigotry has to stand with placid unmoved front against assailants by the hundred. Let us only think of the letters that are addressed to him, of the attacks made upon him, of the questions asked of him.   Against every attack he must defend himself, and yet must he never commit himself.   He must never be dumb, and yet must he never speak out boldly.   He must be always true to the Thirty-nine Articles, and yet never fight for any one of them. In the broad his creed must be infallible, but he himself may make a standing-point on no detail. To carry an archbishop's mitre successfully under such circumstances requires much diligence, considerable skill, imperturbable good humour, and undying patience.

The selections that have been made by the Ministers of the Crown for the last twenty or twenty-five years have all apparently been made on the principle of selecting such archbishops as have been here described, and English Churchmen in general seem to think that the Ministers of the Crown have exercised wise discretion in the appointments which they have made.

II.

ENGLISH BISHOPS, OLD AND NEW.

IF it were said that the difference between bishops of the old school and of the new consists chiefly in the fact that the former wore wigs and that the latter have ceased to do so, the definition would be true enough if it were followed out, not literally, but with a liberal construction. In former days the wig and apron, of themselves, almost sufficed; but now, these outer things having been, to so great an extent, laid aside, other things, much more difficult of acquirement, are needed. There was, however, such an odour of pious decorum round the episcopal wig, that we cannot but regret its departure; and then, again, so much of awe has gone, now that the wig is abandoned! We who can remember the bishops in their full panoply

can hardly understand how a bishop of these times can
be a bishop at all to his subject parsons. And that
veneration which arose from outer circumstances used
to be so peculiarly the perquisite of the bench of
bishops, that men of the laity, thinking over it all,
are at a loss to conceive why appendages so valuable
should have been abandoned thus recklessly. Even
aprons are not worn as aprons were worn of yore,—
but in a shorn degree, showing too plainly that the
reverend wearer is half ashamed of the tranquil
decoration ; and lawn sleeves themselves do not
seem to envelop the occupant in so extensive a
cloud of sacred millinery as they did in the more
reverent days of George the Fourth. Have the
bishops themselves made this suicidal change; or
have they only succumbed to the invincible force of
public opinion in thus abandoning those awful
symbols which were so valuable to them ?

A full and true answer to this question would
go far towards giving a history of the Church of
England during the last sixty or seventy years,—
from the days in which Lord Eldon was first consulted as to the making of a bishop, down to the last

decade of years in which bishops are popularly
supposed to have been selected in accordance with
the advice of a religious Whig nobleman. Such a
history cannot be given here, but the peculiarities of
the old and new bishop may perhaps be so described
as to show something of the result of the changes
that have taken place.

The bishop of George the Third and George the
Fourth was never a prince, as was the archbishop,—
but he was a wealthy ecclesiastical baron, having the
prestige of a Peer of Parliament, even when he did
not use the power, living like a great lord in his
palace, drawing his income from territorial domains,
—an income which was often so much greater than
his needs as to afford him the means of amassing a
colossal fortune. And as he generally entered upon
the possession of this income without any of the
encumbrances which are incidental to the hereditary
possessors of great properties, and usually considered
himself to be precluded by the nature of his profession
from many of those wealth-consuming pursuits to
which his lay brother nobles are prone, it came to
pass that the bishop was ordinarily a rich man. He

kept no race-horses; he was not usually a gambler; he could provide for clerical sons and clerical sons-in-law out of the diocesan pocket : and was preserved by the necessary quiescence of clerical life from that broadcast magnificence which is so costly to our great nobles, because it admits of no check upon its expenditure. The bishop, let him live as handsomely as he might, was not called upon to live beyond the scope of accounts ;—and many of our bishops were good accountants.

But in those halcyon days, there was this drawback to being a bishop, that the good things did not all come at once. What was a bishopric with three thousand a year, when there were others of equal rank with seven, or eight, or occasionally with ten thousand,—not to speak of the sublimity of Canterbury, or the magnificence of York, or the golden opulence of Durham, or the ancient splendour of Winchester, or the metropolitan glory of London ? The interest which made a bishop could translate a bishop, and, therefore, no bishop in those days could rest in comfortable content in the comparatively poor houses of Exeter or Gloucester, while Ely might be reached, or at least Worcester. Thus it came to pass that men, who in those days were never young when they were first chosen, were still living always in hope of some rich change; and that when the rich change came at last, the few remaining years, the wished-for opportunities of wealth, were used with a tenacity of purpose which might almost put a usurer to the blush.

But it would be unreasonable to feel strong abhorrence against the old bishops on this account. Men in all walks of life do as others do around them, and bishops are but men. It was thought to be the proper thing that a bishop should exercise his power over the domains of the see to the utmost extent rendered possible by the existing law. He would run his life against a lease on the ecclesiastical property. If he died before the lease expired the benefit would be to his successor. If he survived he could lease the property for a term of years to his son at a peppercorn rent, and the see would be so far robbed. It was an interesting, exciting mode of life, and as the ecclesiastical lands grew in value as all lands grew,— town lands, for instance, which gradually covered themselves with houses,—the game became so delightful that it is almost a pity that it should have been brought to an end. Let no man say to himself that had he been a bishop in those days he would have done otherwise,— unless he is quite sure that he is better than those around him, even in these days.

But when such good things were going who were the men who got them? And to this may be added a further question, How far did they deserve the good things which were given to them? It used to be said that there were three classes of aspirants to bishoprics, and three ladders by which successful clergymen might place themselves on the bench. There was the editor of the Greek play, whose ladder was generally an acquaintance with Greek punctuation. There was the tutor of a noble pupil, whose ladder was the political bias of his patron. And there was he who could charm the royal ear, whose ladder was as frequently used in the closet as in the pulpit. To these was afterwards added the political aspirant,— the clergyman who could write a pamphlet or advocate a semi-ecclesiastical cause by his spoken or written words.

That scholarship should be remunerated was very well; that men in power should reward those who had been faithful to themselves and their children was, at any rate, very natural; that the Sovereign should occasionally have a voice in making those selections which, as head of the Church, it was popularly supposed that he always made, seemed only to be fair;—and who can say that a Minister was wrong to recompense ecclesiastical support by ecclesiastical preferment? But it must be admitted that the bench of bishops as it was constituted under the circumstances above described was not conspicuous for its clerical energy, for its theological attainments, or for its impartial use of the great church patronage which it possessed. They who sat upon it ordinarily wore their wigs with decorum and lived the lives of gentlemen; but, looking back for many years, a churchman of the Church of England cannot boast of the clerical doings of its bishops. Under the great wig system much of awe was engendered, and that amount of good was attained which consists mainly of respect and reverence for the unknown. The mere existence of a Llama is good for people

who have no more clearly expressed God to worship,
—and in this way the old, rich, bewigged bishops
were serviceable. But, with a few exceptions, they
did but little other clerical service. New churches
were not built under their auspices, nor were old
churches repaired. Dissent in England became
strong, and the services of the State Church were in
many dioceses performed with a laxity and want even
of decency which, though it existed so short a time
since, now hardly obtains belief. The wigs have
gone, but in their places have come,—as we are
bound to acknowledge,—many of those qualities,
much more difficult of acquirement, which men
demand when wigs will no longer satisfy them. Let
any middle-aged man of the present day think of
the bishops of his youth, and remember those who
were known to him by report, repute, or perhaps by
personal intercourse. Although bishops in those
days were not common in the market-places as they
are now, some of us were allowed to see them and
hear them speak, and most of us may have some
memory of their characters. There were the old
bishops who never stirred out, and the young bishops

who went to Court ; and the bishop who was known
to be a Crœsus, and the bishop who had so lived
that, in spite of his almost princely income, he was
obliged to fly his creditors ; and there was the more
innocent bishop who played chess, and the bishop
who still hankered after Greek plays, and the kindly
old bishop who delighted to make punch in moderate
proportions for young people, and a very wicked
bishop or two, whose sins shall not be specially
designated. Such are the bishops we remember,
together with one or two of simple energetic piety.
But who remembers bishops of those days who really
did the work to which they were set ? In how many
dioceses was there a Boanerges of whom the Church
can be proud ? It is almost miraculous that the
Church should have stood at all through such guidance as it has had.

This has now been much altered, and the modern
bishop is at any rate a working man. And while we
congratulate ourselves on the change that has been
made, let us give thanks where thanks are due. No
doubt the increased industry of the bishops has
come, as has the increased industry of public officers,

from the demand of the people whom they are called
upon to serve. But in no way and by no means has
more been done to create this energy than by that
movement at Oxford which had its beginning hardly
more than thirty years since, and of which the two
first leaders are still alive. Dr. Newman has gone to
Rome, and Dr. Pusey has perhaps helped to send
many thither; but these men, and their brethren
of the Tracts, stirred up throughout the country so
strong a feeling of religion, gave rise by their works
to so much thought on a matter which had been
allowed for years to go on almost without any
thought, that it may be said of them that they made
episcopal idleness impossible, and clerical idleness
rare. Of course, it will be said, in opposition to
this, that no school of clergymen has so run after
wiggeries and vestments and empty symbols as have
the followers of the men whom I have named. But
the wiggeries and vestments have been simply the
dross which has come from their fused gold. If you
will make water really boil, some will commonly
boil over. They have built new churches, and
cleansed old churches, and opened closed churches.

They have put on fuel and poked the fire, till heat does really issue from it. It is not only with the High Church,—with their own brethren,—that they have prevailed, but equally with the Low Church, whose handsome edifices and improved services are due to that energy which has been so hateful to them.

The modern bishop is a working man, and he is selected in order that he may work. He is generally one who has been conspicuous as a working parish clergyman, and may be and often is as ignorant of Greek as his former parish clerk. In discussing archbishops it has been said that the chosen candidate must have no strong Church predilections of his own. In choosing a bishop a Minister is bound by no such limit. Perhaps it would be well if High Church, Low Church, and Broad Church could be allowed to have their turns in rotation,—as used to be the case with the two universities. For many years past the Low Church has been in the ascendant, and the chances now are that in meeting a bishop one meets an enemy of the Oxford movement. But the bishop's own predilections matter little, perhaps, if the man will work with a will.   There are few, I think, now who remember much of the Low Church peculiarities of the Bishop of London, having forgotten all that in the results of his episcopate.

But, alas, in losing our fainéant bishops we have lost the great priest lords whom we used to venerate. A bishop now has no domain, but is paid his simple salary of 5,000*l.* a year,—quarterly, we suppose,—and knows not and recks not of leases. He is paid 5,000*l.* a year if his see was in former days worth as much, or less if the see of old was worth less.   London, Durham, and Winchester are more gorgeous than their brethren, but even London and Durham have simple salaries, and Winchester, on the next vacancy, will be reduced to the same humble footing. It is a great fall in worldly state, and consequently bishops may be now seen,—as bishops never were seen of yore,—sitting in cabs, trusting themselves to open one-horse chaises, talking in the market-places, and walking home after an ordination.   These ears have heard and these eyes have seen a modern bishop hallooing from the top of his provincial High-street to a groom who was at the bottom of it, brandishing his episcopal arms the while with an energy which might have been spared. It is so with all things. In seeking for the useful, we are compelled to abandon the picturesque. Our lanes and hedgerows and green commons are all going; and the graceful dignity of the old bishop is a thing of the past.

There still, however, remains to the bench one privilege, which, though shorn of its ancient grandeur of injustice, has in it still much of the sweet mediæval flavour of old English corruption. The patronage of the bishops is as extensive almost as ever; and though its exercise is now hemmed in by certain new stringencies of ecclesiastical law,—as in regard to pluralities, and is also subject to the scrutiny of public opinion, so that decency must at least be respected,—nevertheless patronage remains, as the private property of the bishop. A bishop is not bound, even in theory as the theory at present exists, to bestow his patronage as may be best for the diocese over which he presides. He still gives, and is supposed to give, his best livings to his own friends. A deserving curate has no claim on a bishop for a living as a reward for the work he has done. The peculiarly strong case of a Mr. Cheese may, here and there, give rise to comment; but unless the nepotism is too glaring, nepotism in bishops is allowed ;—nay, it is expected. A bishop's daughter is supposed to offer one of the fairest steps to promotion which the Church of England affords.

Is it not singular that it should be so,—that the idea of giving the fitting reward to the most deserving servant should have to reach the Church the last of all professions and of all trades ? Sinecures and the promotion of young favourites used to be common in the Civil Service ; but the public would not endure it, and the Civil Service has cleansed itself. The army and navy have been subjected to searching reforms. A great law officer has been made to vanish into space because he was too keen in appropriating patronage to family uses. Bankers and brewers will no longer have men about their premises who do not work; and yet bankers and brewers may do what they like with their own. But the bishop, in whose hands patronage has been placed, that he might use it in the holiest way for the highest purpose, still

exercises it daily with the undeniable and acknowledged view of benefiting private friends! And in
doing so he does not even know that he is doing
amiss. It may be doubted whether the bishop has
yet breathed beneath an apron who has doubted that
his patronage was as much his own as the silver
in his breeches-pocket. The bishop's feeling in the
matter is not singular, but it is singular that bishops
should not before this have been enlightened on the
subject of Church patronage by the voice of the laity
whom they serve.

III.

THE NORMAL DEAN OF THE PRESENT DAY.

IF there be any man, who is not or has not been a
Dean himself, who can distinctly define the duties of
a Dean of the Church of England, he must be one
who has studied ecclesiastical subjects very deeply.
When cathedral services were kept up for the honour
of God rather than for the welfare of the worshippers, with an understanding faintly felt by the
indifferent, but strongly realized by the pious, that
recompence would be given by the Almighty for the
honour done to Him,—as cathedrals were originally
built and adorned with that object,—it was natural
enough that there should be placed at the head of
those who served in the choir a high dignitary who,
by the weight of his presence and the grace of his

rank, should give an increased flavour of ecclesiastical excellence to those services. The dean then was the head, as it were, of a college, and he fitly did his work if he looked after the ceremonies of his cathedral, saw that canons, precentor, minor canons and choristers, did their ministrations with creditable grace, took care that the building was, if possible, kept in good repair,—and thus properly took the lead in the chapter over which he presided. But the idea of honouring our Creator by the excellence of our church services, — though it remains firmly fixed enough in the minds of some of us,—is no longer a national idea; and we may say that deans are not selected by those who have the appointment of deans with any such view. We use our cathedrals in these days as big churches, in which multitudes may worship, so that, if possible, they may learn to live Christian lives. They are made beautiful that this worship may be attractive to men, and not for the glory of God. What architect would now think it necessary to spend time and money in the adornment of parts of his edifice which no mortal eye can reach? But such was done in the old days when deans were first instituted. Multitudes, no doubt, crowded our cathedrals in those times, — when bishops and deans were subject to the Pope—but they were there for the honour of God, testifying their faith by the fact of their presence. That all this has been changed need hardly be explained here; but in the change it would seem that the real work of the dean has gone,—except so far as it may please him to take some part in those offices of the church service which it is necessary that a clergyman should perform. It is now ordinarily believed that to the dean is especially entrusted the care of the structure itself; and luckily for us, who love our old cathedrals, we have had some deans of late who, as architectural ecclesiastics, have been very serviceable; but should a dean have no such tendencies,—as many deans have had none,—no penalty for neglect of prescribed duty would fall upon him. A certain amount of yearly residence is enjoined; and it is expected, of course, that a dean should show himself in his own cathedral. Let him reside and show himself, and the city which he graces by his presence will hardly demand from him other services.

In truth, the lines of deans have fallen in pleasant places. Man, being by nature restless and ambitious, desires to rise; and the dean will desire to become a bishop, though he would lose by the change his easy comfort, his sufficient modest home, and the grace of his close in which no one overtops him. To be a Peer of Parliament, to rule the clergy of a diocese, and wear the highest order of clerical vestment, is sweet to the clerical aspirant. A man feels that he is shelved when he ceases to sing excelsior to himself in his closet. But the change from a deanery of the present day to a palace is a change from ease to work, from leisure to turmoil, from peace to war, from books which are ever good-humoured to men who are too often ill-humoured. The dean's modest thousand a year sounds small in comparison with the bishop's more generous stipend:—but look at a dean, and you will always see that he is sleeker than a bishop. The dean to whom fortune has given a quaint old house with pleasant garden in a quaint old close, with resident prebendaries and minor canons around him who just acknowledge, and no more than acknowledge, his superiority,—who takes the lead, as Mr. Dean, in the

society of his clerical city,—who is never called upon
to discharge expensive duties in London, though he
may revisit the glimpses of the metropolitan moon for
a month, perhaps, in the early summer, showing his
new rosette at his club,—seems indeed to have had
his lines given to him in very pleasant places.

There is something charming to the English
ear in the name of the Dean and Chapter. None of
us quite know what it means, and yet we love it.
When we visit our ancient cathedrals, and are taken
into a handsome but manifestly useless octagonal
stone outhouse, we are delighted to find that the
chapter-house is being repaired at an expense of, say,
four thousand pounds, subscribed by the maiden
ladies of the diocese ; or if we find the said outhouse
to be in ruins,—in which case the afflicted verger will
not show it if we allow him to pass easily through
our hands,—we feel a keen regret as though all things
good were going from us. That there should be a
chapter-house attached to the cathedral, simply because a chapter-house was needed in former days, is
all the reason that we can give for our affection ; and
we think that the old ladies have spent their money

well in preserving the relic.   We also think that the
Ecclesiastical Commission spends its money well in
preserving the chapter, and should feel infinite regret
in finding that any diocese had none belonging to it.
We are often told that ours is a utilitarian age, but
this utilitarian spirit is so closely mingled with a
veneration for things old and beautiful from age that
we love our old follies infinitely better than our new
virtues.

Though it is difficult to define the duties of a
modern dean, we all of us know what are the qualities
and what the acquirements which lead to deaneries in
these days; and most of us respect them.   As it is
now necessary that a man shall have been an active
parish parson before he is thought fit to be a bishop,
so it is required that a clergyman shall have shown a
taste for literature in some one of its branches before
he can be regarded among the candidates proper for
a deanery.   The normal dean of this age is a gentleman who would probably not have taken orders
unless the circumstances of his life had placed orders
very clearly in his path.   He is not a man who has
been urged strongly in early youth by a vocation for

clerical duties, or who has subsequently devoted himself to what may be called clerical administrations
proper. He has taken kindly to literature, having
been biassed in his choice of the branch which he has
assumed by the fact of the word " Reverend " which
has attached itself to his name. He has done well
at the university, and has been a fellow, and perhaps
a tutor, of his college. He has written a book or
two, and has not impossibly shown himself to be too
liberal for the bench; for it is given to deans to speak
their thoughts more openly than bishops are allowed
to do. Indeed, this is so well acknowledged a principle in the arrangement of church patronage, that it
has struck many of us with wonder that the Government has not escaped from its difficulty in regard
to the Bishop of Natal by making him a dean in
England.

And, when once a dean, the happy beneficed lover
of letters need make no change in the mode of his
life, as a bishop must do. He is not driven to feel
that now and from henceforth he must have his neck
in a collar to which he has hitherto been unused, and
that he must be drawing ever and always against the

hill. A bishop must do so, or else he is a bad bishop; but a dean has got no hill before him, unless he makes one for himself.

Who that knows any of our dear old closes,—that of Winchester, for instance, or of Norwich, or Hereford, or Salisbury,—has not wandered among the modest, comfortable clerical residences which they contain, envying the lot of those to whom such good things have been given ? The half-sequestered nook has a double delight, because it is only half sequestered. On one side there is an arched gate,—a gate that may possibly be capable of being locked, which gives to the spot a sweet savour of monastic privacy and ecclesiastical reserve ; while on the other side the close opens itself freely to the city by paths leading, probably, under the dear old towers of the cathedral, by the graves of those who have been thought worthy of a resting-place so near the shrine. It opens itself freely to the city, and courts the steps of church matrons, who are almost as clerical as their lords. It is true, indeed, that much of their glory has now departed from these hallowed places. The dean still keeps his deanery, but the number of resident canons has been terribly diminished. Houses intended for church dignitaries are let to prosperous tallow-chandlers, and in the window of a mansion in a close can, at this moment in which I am writing, be seen a notice that lodgings can be had there by a private gentleman—with a reference. But still it is the Close. There is still an odour there to the acutely percipient nostrils as of shovel hats and black vestments. You still talk gently as you walk over its well-kept gravel, and would refrain within its precincts from that strength of language which may perhaps be common to you out in the crowded marts of the city. The cathedral, at any rate, is there, more beautiful than ever,—thanks to the old ladies and the architectural dean. The musical rooks fly above your head. The tower bells delight your ear with those deep-tolling, silence-producing sounds which seem to come from past ages in which men were not so hurried as they are now; and you feel that the resident tallow-chandler and the single gentleman with a reference have not as yet destroyed the ancient piety of the place.

The dean and chapter! How pleasantly the

words sound on the tongue of a reverent verger!
The chapters, I fear, are terribly shorn of their old
glory, and each chapter must look at itself, when it
meets, with something of wistful woe in its half-
extinguished old eyes. And why does a chapter
meet? Its highest duty is a congé d'élire,—permission to choose its own bishop. Permission is
sent down from the Prime Minister to the chapter to
choose Dr. Smith,—a very worthy evangelical gentleman, whose name stinks in the nostrils of the old
high and dry canons and prebendaries who still hang
round the towers of the cathedral; and, — under
certain terrible penalties,—they exercise their functions, and unanimously elect Dr. Smith as the bishop
of that diocese. There must be something melancholy in such moments to a reflective dean and
chapter. We may suppose that the number of
clerical gentlemen who really meet together to carry
on the business of the election is not great. It is
as small, probably, as may be; but something of a
chapter must be held. The ignorant layman, as he
thinks of it, wonders whether the work is really done
in that cold unfurnished octagonal stone building,

which has just been so beautifully repaired at the expense of the devout maiden ladies.

How English, how absurd, how picturesque it all is !— and, we may add, how traditionally useful ! The Queen is the head of the Church, and therefore sends down word to a chapter, which in truth as a chapter no longer exists, that it has permission to choose its bishop, the bishop having been already appointed by the Prime Minister, who is the nominee of the House of Commons ! The chapter makes its choice accordingly, and the whole thing goes on as though the machine were kept in motion by forces as obedient to reason and the laws of nature as those operating on a steam engine. We are often led to express our dismay, and sometimes our scorn, at the ignorance shown by foreigners as to our institutions ; but when we ourselves consider their complications and irrationalistic modes of procedure, the wonder is that any one not to the manner born should be able to fathom aught of their significance.

Deans and chapters, though they exist with a mutilated grandeur, for the present are safe; and long may they remain so !

IV.

THE ARCHDEACON.

A DEAN has been described as a Church dignitary who, as regards his position in the Church, has little to do and a good deal to get. An archdeacon, on the other hand, is a Church dignitary, who in diocesan dignity is indeed almost equal to a dean, and in diocesan power is much superior to a dean, but who has a great deal to do and very little to get. Indeed, as to that matter of getting, the archdeacon,—as archdeacon,—may be said to get almost nothing. It is quite in keeping with the traditional polity and well understood peculiarities of our Church that much work should be required from those officers to whom no payment is allotted, or payment that is next to none; whereas from those to whom affluence is given little labour is required. And the system works well enough. There has as yet been no dearth of archdeacons; nor shall we probably experience any such calamity.

Nevertheless, archdeacons are seldom allowed to starve. The bishops have it in their power to look to that, and knowing that in these days starving men seldom can exercise much authority, they take care that their archdeacons shall be beneficed. The archdeacon always holds a living. In former happy days he not unfrequently held more than one, and there are probably archdeacons still living in that halcyon condition. He always holds a living, and almost always a good living. He not unfrequently is a man of private means, and has been selected for his position partly on that account. He is the nominee of the bishop, and is, therefore, not unfrequently intimately connected with episcopal things. He is, perhaps, the son or nephew of a bishop, or has married a wife from the palace, or has, after some fashion, sat in his early days at episcopal feet. He is one whom the bishop thinks that he can love and trust; and therefore, before he has obtained his archdeaconry, he has probably been endowed with that first requisite for a good servant—good wages. A poor archdeacon, an archdeacon who did not keep a curate or two, an archdeacon who could not give a dinner and put a special bottle of wine upon the table, an archdeacon who did not keep a carriage, or at least a one-horse chaise, an archdeacon without a man servant, or a banker's account, would be no-where,—if I may so speak,—in an English diocese. Such a one could not hold up his head among churchwardens, or inquire as to church repairs with any touch of proper authority. Therefore, though the archdeacon is not paid for his services as arch-deacon, he is generally a gentleman who is well to do in the world, and who can take a comfortable place in the county society among which it is his happy lot to live.

But, above all things, an archdeacon should be a man of the world. He should know well, not only how many shillings there are in a pound, but how many shillings also there are in a clerical pound,—for in these matters there is a difference. Five hundred a year is much more in the hands of a

country parson than it is in the hands of a country
gentleman who is not a parson,—all which the
efficient archdeacon understands and has at his fingers'
ends to the last shilling of the calculation. He
should understand, too, after what fashion his brother
rectors and vicars live around him,—should know
something of their habits, something also of their
means, and should have an eye open to their welfare,
their pursuits, and their amusements. Of all these
things the really stirring archdeacon does in fact
know very much.

The archdeacon is, in fact, a bishop in little, and
as such is often much more of a bishop in fact than
is the bishop himself. To define,—or rather to
make intelligible by any definition,—an archdeacon's
power and duties, would be very difficult ; as also it
is very difficult, or I may say impossible, to do so
with reference to a bishop's functions. The archdeacon holds a court, and makes visitations. These
visitations may be made pretty much at his pleasure.
He must, I believe, make them once in three years,
but may make them every year if he thinks fit. He
inquires as to the administration of the services,

seeing that the canons are maintained, but has no power to alter aught ; and as there seems to be much difficulty in knowing when and by what the canons are maintained, and when and by what they are not maintained, we may imagine that the inquiries of a discreet archdeacon into the practices of a respectable and efficient parson will not be too close or searching in this matter of the canons.   It is, however, easier to see whether the windows of a church are in repair, and whether the roof keeps out the rain, than it is to be intelligibly and efficiently explicit on the subject of canons, and, therefore, the outward structure of the parish church gives very safe employment to an archdeacon.   The little difficulty as to church rates which sometimes follows upon an order for repairs is not uncongenial to the archdeacon's mind.   It hinges upon politics, and upon a vexed political question in which the archdeacon, as a strong local Conservative, has hitherto had his victories.   There remain so very few subjects which are still grateful to him in the same way, that church rates, with all their little impediments and embargoes, naturally present themselves to him as pleasant matters.   And then the archdeacons receive reports from the churchwardens, if churchwardens have anything to report,—any scandal of which to tell, or evil practices on the parson's side of which complaint has unfortunately become necessary according to the judgment of those churchwardens ! By the word " scandal " let not the uninitiated reader be led to think that undignified tittle-tattle with his neighbour's churchwardens is the duty or the employment of an archdeacon. Open moral misconduct in a clergyman's life is supposed to be matter of justifiable public scandal—the scandal arising with the clerical sinner, and not with those who tell of the sin—and, as such, is, by the constitution of our Church, an especial subject for the care of our archdeacons, and indeed, under them, of our churchwardens. But in such matters archdeacons are liberal, and much prefer to wink an eye than to see too much. We may imagine that a church-warden, misunderstanding his mission with regard to scandal, and taking upon himself too promptly the duty of watching the moral conduct of his parson, would not receive much comfort from a visiting arch-deacon. No one knows better than an archdeacon—

no one knows so well as an archdeacon—that it is needless and absurd to look for a St. Paul in every parsonage. He would, indeed, be very little at his own ease with a local St. Paul, much preferring a comfortable rector, who can take his glass of wine after dinner and talk pleasantly of old college days. St. Pauls, however, do not trouble him ; nor is he troubled much by the scandals of his clerical neighbours ; but he must be troubled sorely, I should think, by the increasing number and increasing influence around him of those " literate " clergymen who—from want of better, as we must in sorrow confess,—are flocking to us from Islington, Birkenhead, and such like fountains of pastoral care. The man who won't drink his glass of wine, and talk of his college, and put off for a few happy hours the sacred stiffnesses of the profession and become simply an English gentleman,—he is the clergyman whom in his heart the archdeacon does not love.

Thus the archdeacon is a bishop in little as regards his own archdeaconry, which may probably comprise half a diocese ; and as an energetic financial secretary at the Treasury may, under an uninstructed

Chancellor of the Exchequer, have much more to do with the finances of the country than the Chancellor of the Exchequer himself, so may an energetic archdeacon have a much stronger influence on his clerical district than the bishop who is over him. He is the bishop's eye, or should be so, and may not improbably become the bishop's hand.

But the archdeacon, in spite of all his power and authority, though he be so great among his brother parsons, is hardly in the way to better promotion. High promotion in the Church now comes from political influence or from the friendship of Ministers, —from those things, combined of course with high clerical attainments—and an archdeacon is not often in the way to obtain political influence or the friendship of Ministers. As deans live in towns, so do archdeacons live in the country; and like other country gentlemen they are always in opposition. And then they are men who have been made what they are by the bishops, and, therefore, are known well in their dioceses, but are not much known beyond them. They culminate in their own local dignity, and, knowing that they do so, they make

the most of it. An archdeacon who is potent with
his bishop, and who is popular with his clergymen,
who works hard and can do so without undue
meddling, who has a pleasant parish of his own and
is not troubled by ambitious or indifferent curates,
who can live on good terms with the squires around
him, understanding how far it is expedient that he
should be restricted by his coat, and how far he may
go in discarding hyper-clerical constraint, is master
of a position in which he need not envy the success
of any professional gentleman in the kingdom. But
he is not on the direct road to higher things, and
will probably die in his rectory, an archdeacon to
the last.

If an archdeacon be ambitious of moving in higher
clerical matters than his archdeaconry affords him,
he generally looks to gratify that desire by sitting in
Convocation. This method of doing something more
than routine duty is easier and less likely to fail than
the other method of publishing a volume of sermons.
Sermons are not read now as they were some thirty
or forty years since, and Convocation has lately held
its head a little up, obtaining recognition in the

newspapers, and appearing to do something. An archdeacon is just the man to believe that Convocation can do much; and this faith on his part is evidence of a moral freshness and a real earnestness which adds a charm to his normal character. Who can bring himself to believe that a bishop believes in Convocation—a bishop, that is, who takes his seat in the House of Lords, talks to other peers, and knows what is going on in the well-instructed blasé London world? Such a one cannot but see, cannot but know, that Convocation is a clerical toy, a mere debating society to which belongs none of the vitality of power. But the archdeacon, fresh from the country, believes in Convocation, and works there with some real conviction that he is one of a clerical Parliament, and that he is animated by true parliamentary life.

But it is in his own rectory that an archdeacon must ever shine with the brightest light. I have said that he is a bishop in little, and I may also say that he is the very chief among parsons; and as the country parson—the country parson with pleasant parsonage, pleasanter wife, and plenty of children— is the true and proper type of an English clergyman, to which bishops, deans, canons, and curates are mere adjuncts and necessary excrescences, so is the archdeacon the highest type of the country parson. He is always married—an exception here or there would but prove the rule—he generally has a large family; of course he has a pleasant rectory. He must be an earnest working parish clergyman, or he would hardly have been selected as an archdeacon. He is necessarily—I may say certainly—a gentleman. Alas! that the day should have gone by when the same might have been said of every clergyman bearing orders in the Church of England. He is a man of the world, as I have above explained, and as such it is not probable that he will be a fanatic, though living examples may probably be adduced that fanaticism can exist under an archdeacon's hat. And he walks just a head taller than other clergymen around him, receiving that pleasant attitude from the modest authority which he carries. Of all attitudes it is the most pleasant. He who stands high on a column can hardly talk pleasantly with those who stand round his pedestal; and that haranguing with loud voice from column top to column top is but a cold ceremonial conversation. Who can imagine two archbishops slapping each other's backs and being jolly together? But an archdeacon is not raised by his dignity above a capability for jovial intimacy, and yet he walks with his head pleasantly raised above the heads of other parsons around him.

V.

THE PARSON OF THE PARISH.

THE word parson is generally supposed to be a slang
term for the rector, vicar, or incumbent of a parish,
and, in the present day, is not often used without
some intended touch of drollery,—unless by the rustics
of country parishes who still cling to the old word.
But the rustics are in the right, for of all terms by
which clergymen of the Church of England are known,
there is none more honourable in its origin than that
of parson. By that word the parish clergyman is
designated as the palpable and visible personage of
the church of his parish, making that by his presence
an intelligible reality which, without him, would be
but an invisible idea. Parsons were so called before
rectors or vicars were known, and in ages which had
heard nothing of that abominable word incumbent.
A parson proper, indeed, was above a vicar,—who

originally was simply the curate of an impersonal parson, and acted as priest in a parish as to which some abbey or chapter stood in the position of parson. The title of rector itself is new-fangled in comparison with that of parson, and has no special ecclesiastical significance. The parson, properly so called, had not only the full charge of his parish, but the full benefit derivable from the tithes ; and then he came to change his name and to be called politely a rector. The vicar was he who had the full charge of his parish, as also he has at present, vicariously at first for some abbey or chapter ; and now, in these days, vicariously for some lay improprietor, — but who had and has the benefit only of the so-called small tithes ; and then he also came to be called the parson. Rectors and vicars at present hold their livings by tenures which are equally firm, and they have done so now for more than four hundred years. The rustics above mentioned would be much surprised if told that their vicar was not a real parson. In speaking, therefore, of the parson of the parish, let us be understood to mean the parish clergyman, who has that full fruition of his living which is given by freehold possession.

There is a pleasant flavour of old crusted port present to the palate of one's imagination when mention is made of a rector, which he misses perhaps in inquiring after the vicar, whose beer may be better than his wine; and the rector cuts lustily from the haunch, while the vicar is scientific with the shoulder. But we expect, on the other hand, and are gratified in expecting, a kinder and more genial flow of clerical wit from the vicar than the rector gives us; and I have generally found the vicar's armchair to be easier than that of his elder brother. But here, in speaking of the English parson,—of the priest who has full clerical command in his parish,—no distinction between rector and vicar shall be made.

The parson of the parish is the proper type and most becoming form of the English clergyman as the captain of his ship is of the English naval officer. Admirals of the Red and Admirals of the Blue, and Commodores with authority ashore, are very fine fellows, and may perhaps be greater in their way than the captain can be in his; but for real naval efficiency and authority the captain of the ship on his own quarter-deck stands unequalled. And so it is with the parson of the parish in his own glebe. He is pure parson and nothing else, and in the daily work of his life, if he does that daily work diligently, he cannot but feel that he is devoting himself to those duties which properly belong to him. Whether a bishop in the House of Lords may so think of himself, or a bishop speaking from a platform, or a bishop in the turmoils of correspondence, or even a bishop dispensing his patronage, may be more doubtful. And the easy dean may doubt whether such ease was intended for him when he took upon himself to bear the arms of St. Paul. And the fellow of a college, even though he be tutor as well as fellow, may feel some qualms as to that word reverend with which he has caused the world to address him. But the parson in his parish must know that he has got himself into that place for which he has been expressly fitted by the orders he has taken. The curate, who is always a curate, to whom it is never given to exercise by his own right the highest clerical authority in his parish, cannot be said to have fulfilled the mission of his profession satisfactorily, let him have worked ever so nobly. He is as the lieutenant who never rises to be a captain. But the parson requires no further exaltation for clerical excellence. The higher he rises above parsondom, the less will he be of a clergyman. He may become a peer of Parliament, or the head of a chapter, or a local magistrate over other clergymen, as is an archdeacon; but as simply parish parson, he fills the most clerical office in his profession.

The parson of the parish in England, a few years since, was almost' necessarily a man who had been educated at Oxford or Cambridge. An English parish might indeed have an Irishman from Trinity College, Dublin; and, now and again, an outsider was admitted into the fold as a shepherd. There was a small college in the north to fit northern candidates for northern congregations, and the rule was not absolutely absolute; but it prevailed so far that it was felt to be a rule. And thence came an assurance, in which trust was put more or less by all classes, that the parson of the parish was at least a gentleman. He was a man who had lived on equal terms with the highest of the land in point of birth, and hence arose a feeling that was very general in rural parishes, and as salutary as it was general, that the occupant of the parsonage was as good a man as the occupant of the squire's house. It would be interesting to us to trace when this feeling first became common, knowing as we do know that for many years after the Reformation, and down even to a comparatively late date, the rural clergyman was anything but highly esteemed. We are told constantly that the parson left the dining-room when the pudding came in, and that he by no means did badly for himself in marrying the lady's maid. We most of us know the character of that eminent divine Dr. Tusher, who lived in the reign of Queen Anne. Then came the halcyon days of British clergymen,— the happy days of George III. and George IV., and the parson in his parsonage was as good a gentleman as any squire in his mansion or nobleman in his castle. There is, alas! a new order of things coming on us which threatens us with some changes, not for the better, in this respect. There are theological colleges here and there, and men and women talk of "literates." Who shall dare to say that it may not all be for the best? Who will venture to prophesy that there shall be less energetic teaching of God's word under the new order of things than under the old? But, as to the special man of whom we speak now, the English parish parson, with whom we all love to be on familiar terms,—that he will be an altered man, and as a man less attractive, less urbane, less genial,—in one significant word, less of a gentleman,—that such will be the result of theological colleges and the institution of "literates," no one who has thought of the subject will have any doubt.

And in no capacity is a gentleman more required or more quickly recognized than in that of a parson. Who has not seen a thrifty household mistress holding almost unconsciously between her finger and thumb a piece of silk or linen, and telling at once by the touch whether the fabric be good? This is done with almost an instinct in the matter, and habit has made perfect in the woman that which was born with her. Exactly in the same way, only much more unconsciously, will the English rustic take his new parson between his finger and thumb and find out whether he be a gentleman. The rustic cannot tell by what law he judges, but he knows the article, and the

gentleman he will obey and respect, in the gentleman
he will believe. Such is his nature. While in the
other, who has not responded favourably to the touch
of the rustic's finger, the rustic will not believe, nor
by him will he be restrained, if restraint be necessary.
The rustic in this may show, perhaps, both his ignorance and servility, as well as the skilled power of
his fingering,—but such is his nature.

But the adult parson of the parish in England,—
the clergyman who has reached, if I may so say, the
full dominion of his quarter-deck,—is still customarily
a man from Oxford or from Cambridge, and it is of
such a one that we speak here. He has probably
been the younger son of a squire, or else his father
has been a parson, as he is himself. Throughout
his whole life he has lived in close communion
with rural affairs, and has of them that exact knowledge which close communion only will give. He
knows accurately, from lessons which he has learned
unknowingly, the extent of the evil and the extent of
the good which exists around him, and he adapts
himself to the one and to the other. Against gross
profligacy and loud sin he can inveigh boldly, and he

can make men and women to shake in their shoes
by telling them of the punishment which will follow
such courses; but with the peccadilloes dear to the
rustic mind he knows how to make compromises, and
can put up with a little drunkenness, with occasional
sabbath-breaking, with ordinary oaths, and with
church somnolence. He does not expect much of
poor human nature, and is thankful for moderate
results. He is generally a man imbued with strong
prejudice, thinking ill of all countries and all
religions but his own; but in spite of his prejudices
he is liberal, and though he thinks ill of men, he
would not punish them for the ill that he thinks.
He has something of bigotry in his heart, and would
probably be willing, if the times served his purpose,
to make all men members of the Church of England
by Act of Parliament; but though he is a bigot, he
is not a fanatic, and as long as men will belong to his
Church, he is quite willing that the obligations of
that Church shall sit lightly upon them. He loves
his religion and wages an honest fight with the devil;
but even with the devil he likes to deal courteously,
and is not averse to some occasional truces. He is

quite in earnest, but he dislikes zeal; and of all men whom he hates, the over-pious young curate, who will never allow ginger to be hot in the mouth, is the man whom he hates the most. He carries out his Bible teaching in preferring the publican to the Pharisee, and can deal much more comfortably with an occasional backslider than he can with any man who always walks, or appears to walk, in the straight course.

It almost seems that something approaching to hypocrisy were a necessary component part of the character of the English parish parson, and yet he is a man always on the alert to be honest. It is his misfortune that he must preach higher than his own practice, and that he is driven to pretend to think that a stricter course of life is necessary than that which he would desire to see followed out even in his own family. As the mealman in the description of his flours can never go below "middlings," knowing that they who wish to get the cheapest article would never buy it if it were actually ticketed as being of the worst quality, so is the parson driven to ticket all his articles above their real value. He cannot tell his people what amount of religion will really suffice for them, knowing that he will never get from them all that he asks ; and thus he is compelled to have an inner life and an outer,—an inner life, in which he squares his religious views with his real ideas as to that which God requires from his creatures ; and an outer life, in which he is always demanding much in order that he may get little. From this it results that a parish parson among his own friends differs much from the parish parson among his parishioners, and that he is always, as it were, winking at those who know him as a man, while he is most eager in his exercitations among those who only know him as a clergyman.

The parish parson generally has a grievance, and is much attached to it,—in which he is like all other men in all other walks of life. He not uncommonly maintains a mild opposition to his bishop, upon whom he is apt to look down as belonging to a new order of things, and whom he regards, on account of this new order of things, as being not above half a clergyman. As he rises in years and repute he becomes a rural dean, and exercises some small authority out of his own parish, by which, however, his character as a parish parson, pure and simple, is somewhat damaged. He is great in the management of his curate, and arrives at such perfection in his professional career that he inspires his clerk with mingled awe and affection.

Such is the English parish parson, as he was almost always some fifty years since, as he is still in many parishes, but as he will soon cease to become. The homes of such men are among the pleasantest in the country, just reaching in well-being and abundance that point at which perfect comfort exists and magnificence has not yet begun to display itself. And the men themselves have no superiors in their adaptability to social happiness. How pleasantly they talk when the room is tiled, and the outward world is shut out for the night! How they delight in the modest pleasures of the table, sitting in unquestioned ease over a ruddy fire, while the bottle stands ready to the grasp, but not to be grasped too frequently or too quickly. Methinks the eye of no man beams so kindly on me as I fill my glass for the third time after dinner as does the eye of the parson of the parish.

VI.

THE TOWN INCUMBENT.

Dr. Johnson tells us that an incumbent is he who is in present possession of a benefice, and by quoting Swift shows us that, though in possession of a benefice, the incumbent may be in possession of very little benefit from his benefice. "In many places," Swift says, as quoted by Johnson, "the whole ecclesiastical dues are in lay hands, and the incumbent lieth at the mercy of his patron." The word, therefore, is legitimately used in its ecclesiastical sense, and can apparently be legitimately used in no other sense; but, nevertheless, it has no pleasantly ecclesiastical flavour, and carries with itself none of that acknowledged right to respect which is attached to other clerical titles. To be named as a curate is almost better than to be named as an incumbent; for the curate is supposed to be young, and is on his proper road to higher church grades, whereas the incumbent is one who has obtained his promotion, but who is, after all, only an—incumbent. Every parish parson in the kingdom is no doubt an incumbent, but in ordinary parlance we hardly apply the name to the country rector or to the vicar blessed with a pleasant parsonage. The incumbent, as we generally recognize him, is a clergyman who has obtained a town district, who has a church of his own therein from whence he draws what income he may make, chiefly by the letting of sittings, and is so called simply because no other clerical title seems properly to belong to him. No clerical aspirant would be an incumbent,—so to be called,— who could become a parson proper.

The town incumbent, therefore, is rarely a man well to do in the world. He is one who earns his bread hardly in the sweat of his brow, and too often earns but very poor bread. It is not he who has married or who will marry the bishop's daughter. Indeed, before he becomes a town incumbent he has generally put himself beyond such promotion as that by marrying the girl of his heart without a penny. Had he not done so, and thus become terribly in want of an income,—an income at once, though it be a small income,—he would not have taken a district church, and have submitted his neck to the yoke of town incumbency. He knows that in doing so he is consenting to place himself in that branch of his profession which is the least honoured, though not perhaps the least honourable. He is subjecting himself to the heaviest clerical work with but a small prospect of large clerical loaves or fine clerical fishes; and he is prepared to live in a much lower social rank than that which is enjoyed by his more fortunate brothers in the country. The country parson is all but the squire's equal,—is below the squire in parish standing only as a younger brother is below his elder; but the town incumbent is not equal to the town mayor, and in the estimation of many of his fellow-townsmen is hardly superior to the town beadle. Indeed, he is too often simply recognized as the professional gentleman who has taken his family into the last built new house in

Albert Terrace. There, in Albert Terrace, he looks out upon a brickfield, and writes his sermons with very little of that prestige which belongs to the genuine British parson of the parish. His flock are his hearers, not his parishioners. They sit under him, some because his district church of St. Mary is the nearest to them, some because the sittings at St. Mary's are 5s. 6d. a year cheaper than they are at the next place of worship,—for St. Mary's is a place of worship rather than a church to the minds of the townsmen,—and some because they prefer his preaching to the preaching of another town incumbent. They sit under him, but they are not his people jure divino, for him to deal with them concerning their eternal welfare as he may please. He does not even know the name of the man who lives next door to him in Albert Terrace; whereas the true parson of the parish knows every detail as to every child born within his domain. The one is simply the town incumbent of St. Mary's as another man may be an attorney, and a third an apothecary; whereas the rural parson is the personage of his parish.

To the position of the town incumbent are attached none of those half-barbarous but picturesque circumstances which still make the position of our country parsons almost unintelligible to the inquiring foreigner. One clergyman, with little or nothing to do in his parish, has fifteen hundred a year and a beautiful house for doing that little,—which after all is done by a curate ; while his neighbour in the next parish with four times the area and eight times the population, receives one hundred and fifty pounds a year in lieu of the little tithes ! And yet neither does the one feel himself to have been unduly favoured, nor does the other think himself to be injured ! Such are the more-than-half-barbarous, but still picturesque circumstances of our rural parishes. But there is nothing either barbarous or picturesque about the town incumbent. He has allotted to him a district, with such or such a population,—a certain number of thousands over whom it must be much beyond his power to achieve anything approaching to a pastoral surveillance,—with a church in the middle of it, and an income which will fluctuate as the seats in it may be full or empty. Here, in this arrangement, all the principles of political economy are kept in view. Here are supply and demand. Those who want him will come to him and pay him,—as they do to the baker or the dentist. If they don't think he suits them, they will leave him,—as also in similar circumstances they leave their baker and their dentist. If he can fill his church he will live well and become sleek. If his gifts in preaching are small, or if his piety be unrecognized and his labours disregarded, he will live badly and his outward man will become rusty. Among town incumbents the rusty greatly exceed the sleek in numbers.

The town incumbent of whom we are here speaking generally finds himself located among the growing outskirts of a manufacturing town. Here he sees the world increasing around him with wonderful rapidity, and sees also much of the success of the world. The man who began his struggle in life as a manufacturer, when he, the incumbent, also began his struggle, soon rises from step to step, adding chimney to chimney, and buys his villa residence and sets up his carriage. In his career, failure was, of course, possible, but the road to success was open to him, and has been quickly reached. This his neighbour, the clergyman, sees, and tells himself, not without bitterness, that for him there is no such road. For him there must always be poverty and hard work, —that worst of all poverty which has to hide itself under a black coat, and work which is not only ceaseless, but too often thankless and apparently without adequate result! This must be his lot in life, he tells himself,—unless he can preach himself into a reputation. If he can do that, if he can be a M'Neale or an English Ward Beecher, then, indeed, there will be a career open to him. Then he will be sleek, and people will ask him to dinner, and the wife of his bosom will hold up her head among other dames, and his name will become familiar in the columns of newspapers. This after all is what men want, town incumbents as well as others ; and so the town incumbent sets himself to work to make a reputation for himself by pulpit eloquence. As he walks along the dull new streets of his district he fills himself with this ambition, and declares to himself that he will be great as a preacher. He will fill his seats, and draw men to him, —or, if not men, at least women. He will denounce sins with a loud voice and eager accents. And he will denounce not only sins, but heresies also, and lax doctrines. By denouncing simply sin few clerical aspirants have become noted among their neighbours, but the man who will denounce his neighbours' opinions as well as his sins will become famous. And so the town incumbent settles himself to his desk and goes to work.

It will be said, no doubt, that a monstrous accusation is here brought against a body of men who are very eager in doing good works. It is not meant as any accusation. No charge is intended to be made against town incumbents, or against any clergyman, in the description here given. They endeavour simply to succeed in their profession, as every man blessed with activity will attempt to succeed in his profession if it be one in which there is room for success. Given the church to fill, and the incumbency to be made valuable by filling it, and it is simply human nature that an energetic man shall endeavour to fill his church and make his profession valuable. He cannot fill his church by visiting the poor. He cannot earn for himself

even a decent position in the district in which he
lives by a careful performance of ordinary clerical
duties. If he simply reads the services and officiates
at the communion table, and preaches drowsy sermons, he will starve on some 200*l.* a year, and never
get his head above water, either as regards money
or reputation. Of course he will do his best for
himself, and of course he will teach himself to believe
that in doing so he is doing the best for the cause
which he really loves in his heart. He is not a bad
man, or a hypocrite, because he denounces heresies
and lax doctrines in a loud voice, instead of endea-
vouring to teach his people simply that they should
not lie, or get drunk, or steal. He is probably a
very good man; but he is a good man who would
like to have 1,000*l.* a year and a name, instead of
200*l.* a year and no name at all.

But he probably fails. It is sad to say it, and sad
to think of it, but failure is the ordinary lot of man.
A few among us do advance far enough in the
accomplishment of their aspirations to merit the
reputation of success, and they are heard of in the
world; but the mass of men strive for a while to

do something, and then sink down into the common
ruck, finding the struggle to be too hard for them.
They earn bread and live ; and at last, perhaps, are
contented. So it is with the town incumbent. He
preaches for a while with all his force. He spends
sleepless nights in the composition of his sermons.
He becomes bolder and bolder in his denouncings.
But it is of no avail. He has not the gift of pouring
forth either honey or liquid fire from his lips, and
his energy is all wasted. He throws himself in
despair on the bosom of his wife, who alone has
believed in him, and declares that his people have
adders' ears and hearts of stone. From that time
forth, with saddened spirit and heart all sick within
him, he trudges on upon his daily round of duties,
not cursing the day, but reviling the day with an
asperity purely clerical, on which he became—a town
incumbent.

But it is possible that he does not fail. There
are, no doubt, town incumbents who succeed in
preaching themselves into fortunes and reputations,
and who become very sleek and very famous, who are
able to mount higher than their pulpits, on to plat-

forms, and can then enjoy the inestimable privilege of abusing their opponents without fear of reply. But, of all clergymen, the successful town preacher seems to be the farthest removed from those clerical excellences of charity and good-will among men, and the farthest also from those special clerical duties for which our clergy are most valued. They will preach;—yes, by the hour together! Nine times a week we have heard of such a one preaching, and have then known him to speak of himself as a martyr in the service! But they will do nothing else.

For the unsuccessful town incumbent we all of us have sympathy. His work is hard, his payment is small, and his lines have fallen to him in unpleasant places. But for the successful town incumbent, for the clergyman who fills his church with prayerful, tearful, excitable, but at the same time remunerative ladies, few men can have any sympathy.

The position of the town incumbent is not, in truth, in unison with the Church of England as established among us. The glory of the English parson is that his position is ensured to him whether he satisfies those whom he is called upon to serve,

or whether he does not satisfy them. Consequently
he can be, and is, independent of his congregation.
He will wish of course to be on pleasant terms with
them, but it will not be for his pocket's sake. And
it seems that such independence as this is essential
to the position of a clergyman of the Church of
England. It is doubtless true that the number of
rural rectors and vicars among us will never be
increased, whereas the number of town incumbents
will continue to increase from year to year. As the
population grows, so will their number grow. But
it is to be hoped that the peculiar evils of their
position may be remedied by altered arrangements as
to their income. If this be not possible, or be not
done, we shall hardly find that sons of English
gentlemen will continue to seek the Church as a
profession.

VII.

THE COLLEGE FELLOW WHO HAS TAKEN ORDERS.

In speaking of a college fellow, a fellow of a college at Oxford or Cambridge is the fellow of whom we intend to speak. There may, probably, be other fellowships going in these prolific days, as there are other universities, and degrees given by other academical bodies; but we will claim, for the moment, to belong to the old school in such matters, and will recognize as college fellows only those who are presented to us as fellows by the two great sister universities.

When a man becomes a fellow various possessions and privileges are conferred upon him, such as a certain income, a certain rank in his college, a residence within his college, and a place at the high table in hall; and among these privileges and possessions is the great privilege — of a title to orders. In respect to some fellowships this privilege may be enjoyed or neglected according to the will of the individual fellow. In respect to others the fellow must avail himself of it, and must become a clergyman, if not absolutely at once, then within a short period of his election. And there is a third condition, such as that which prevails at the greatest of all our colleges, namely, Trinity, Cambridge, in accordance with which certain years of grace are allowed, and a fellow may remain a fellow for a period of years without taking orders. But, as we believe, at all these colleges a fellowship confers a title to orders,—the right, that is, on the part of the fellow to demand ordination from the bishop; and, as a rule, this privilege is enjoyed. As we are dealing in these sketches with none but clergymen, the fellow who has availed himself of this title is the fellow whom we will keep in view.

All our readers will know what is meant by taking orders,—the process by which a layman becomes a deacon or a priest under the bishop's hands; and most of them will understand that a title to orders is the possession in prospect of such sacerdotal position as will justify a bishop in turning a layman into a clergyman. Thus, for instance, a man has a title to orders who can show that there is a living waiting for his enjoyment and for his services. The offer of a curacy confers a title, and this is the title by which the great body of aspirants to the sacerdotal profession claim their right to admission. Such claimants the bishop is bound to ordain, providing that they show themselves to be fit;—but without a title, or recognized place of clerical duty ready for the candidate as soon as he shall become a clergyman, no bishop will ordain any one. And among other titles there is the title conferred by a college fellowship. The fellow of a college goes before a bishop demanding to be ordained simply because he is a fellow,—and the bishop ordains him. It is a great privilege, for that man is Reverend from that time forth for evermore. In all future ages he will be written down as having been Reverend.

There can be no doubt that when this pleasant arrangement became a portion of college law there was good reason for it. The colleges were ecclesiastical bodies, generally if not entirely under ecclesiastical governance, and a fellow not an ecclesiastic would have been very much in the way at most of them. Men who were clergymen, and men who were not, differed much more strongly then than they do now, both as to the inner life of the man and the outward appearance of the man. And it was then recognized as a part of the great Church system of the day, that in many places ecclesiastics, who were of course unmarried, should live together, passing their time in that state which was then considered to be for them the most salutary and to others the most useful,—saying prayers for the laity which the laity could hardly be got to say for themselves, and maintaining by their continued presence at the universities something of the result of their education, and some show of learning and piety. In those days the fellows of our colleges were monks of a favoured order,—especially favoured because they were, or were presumed to be, especially learned. Looking at our Church, our colleges, and our religion, as they then existed, we shall feel little doubt as to the propriety of fellows having been clergymen in those days. But now,—now that things are so much altered in our Church and in our colleges and in our religion,—sometimes a doubt does creep upon us as to the expediency of this title to orders which a fellowship conveys, and the use which is made of this title.

In the Roman Catholic Church worship seems to have been ordained for the gratification of God. The people were, and indeed are still, taught that God and his saints like prayers and incense and church services, and will reward those who are liberal in bestowing them. It is, therefore, natural that in the Church of Rome there should be,—or, more natural still, that there should have been when this idea was more prevalent in Roman Catholic countries than it is now,—legions of priests whose church administrations were performed with a view to their effect on the Creator, and with no view to any effect on man. But in Protestant countries worship is used, as we suppose, simply for the use of man. It is the duty of the clergyman, as clergyman, to assist other men in worshipping rather than to achieve anything by worship on his own part. If such be the case,—and such appears to be at any rate the existing theory of our own Protestant Church,—it is difficult to conceive how any man can become a clergyman of the Church of England who has no intention whatsoever of helping others to worship,—who has not before him any prospect of performing the duties of a clergyman.

It will be said, doubtless, that the statement here made is wrong and untrue, because the clerical fellow of a college has always before him the prospect of succeeding to a college living, and does generally end his days as the parson of a parish to which he has been presented by his college in the regular order of good things accruing to him. It is quite true that the clerical fellow does in this way become a real clergyman, or a parson proper if I may so call him, in the latter half of his life, when at forty or forty-five he begins to feel that he would like to have something softer near to him than his gyp or laundrywoman, and bethinks himself of some Eliza whom he has long half loved, but would never before allow himself

to love altogether,—because of his fellowship. The
fellow then drops his fellowship, and takes a living,
and goes to his parish and becomes a real clergyman.
But the fact that he does so offers only another and
a stronger objection to his original ordination, while
it does not, in truth, at all invalidate that already
stated.   It is true that the fellow becomes a clergyman at last; but who will maintain that any man has
fitly used a profession to which he has never applied
himself during those years of his life in which his
energy was the strongest, and which he embraced
without any view to using it at all?   The fellow
of a college is ordained in order that he may hold
his fellowship, — because in old days, when the
fellowship was instituted, fellows were supposed to
live the life of monks.   We do not think that any
existing fellow of a college at Oxford or Cambridge
will declare that he has undergone ordination with
an express view to the living to which he may
succeed after ten or fifteen years.

And now we will venture to say a few words as to
that stronger objection to the practice of ordaining
fellows which we maintain is to be found in this

practice of their succeeding to college livings by rotation. When we employ a doctor or a lawyer or an architect, we select a man who knows his profession, and who has proved that he knows it by his practice. Young men entering these professions make their way upwards to that reputation which will bring them practice by attaching themselves to those who are older and more experienced, or by consenting to practise for a while, as it were, experimentally, without much view to income. And in the Church generally the same order of things prevails. It is admitted on all hands within the church, by bishops, by archdeacons, by all working parish clergymen,—by all men who have interested themselves on the subject,—that the only fit education for a parish parson is to be found in a parish curacy. As a man to be a good bishop should have been a parish parson, so to be a good parson a man should have been a curate. That we take to be good clergyman's law; but that law is infringed on every occasion on which a college living is taken by a resident college fellow. A college fellow may, of course, become a curate, and when such a one succeeds to his living all is well. But the man who does so should have been ordained on the title of his curacy, not on the title of his fellowship.

Does any man believe that that very pleasant fellow whom he has known at college, and who has sparkled so brightly in common room, who has been so energetic in the management of the college finances, and in the reform of college abuses,—who has gradually succeeded during his fifteen years of residence in putting off all those outward clerical symbols which as a novice he found himself constrained to adopt, and who during his annual visit to London has become a well-instructed man of the world,—can any one, we say, believe that such a one at the age of forty can be fit to go into a parish and undertake the cure of the parochial souls? There are, we fancy, some who do so believe; but they are those who think that nothing is necessary to make a parson but orders and a living,—that the profession of a clergyman is unlike any other trade or calling known, requiring for the due performance of its duties no special fitness, no training, no skill, no practice, no thought, and no preparation.

The Reverend Joseph Brown stands senior on the list of the fellows of St. Lazarus, within the walls of which happy institution he has lived as fellow and bursar for the last thirty years. No man understands better than the Reverend Joseph Brown the proper temperature of port wine, or the amount of service which a college servant should render. But at the age of fifty-five he falls into unexpectedly tender relations with an amiable female, and on that account he undertakes the pastoral care of the souls of the parish of Eiderdown! What if Eiderdown got its doctor in the same way, or its butcher? What if the ladies of Eiderdown were bound to employ a milliner sent to them after some such fashion? But no man or woman can conceive the possibility of any workman presuming to attempt to earn his bread by his work after such a fashion as this,—excepting always a clergyman. In the Church, because it is so picturesque and well-beloved in its old-fashioned garments, we can put up with anomalies which elsewhere would be unendurable. A bishop uses his patronage as personal property, and college fellows become clergymen and succeed to livings by right, as though in this business of the cure of souls, and in this business only, there were no necessity for that progress in skill and efficiency which all other callings demand ! There was a time when men became captains of ships and colonels of regiments in much the same way ; but the picturesque absurdities of the army and navy were less endearing than those of the Church, and they therefore have been made to succumb.

It will probably be admitted that the Reverend Joseph Brown, much as he was liked by all who knew him at St. Lazarus, and much as he was respected by those who were brought into collegiate relations with him, was not the very best pastor whom the Church of England could have given to the people of Eiderdown ; but many who will admit this will still think that in being ordained as a young man on the title of his fellowship, he did that which was becoming to him as one who had passed through his university education with honour and success. Fellows of colleges always have been clergymen, holding high characters as such in their profession, and why not the Reverend Joseph Brown ? Is it not

also known to us that such a man, located as a
bachelor in his college, is more likely to lead a good
and sober life as a clergyman than he would do as a
layman ? Such, probably, would be the arguments
used in defence of clerical fellowships ; and we will
admit that the Reverend Joseph Brown has throughout his whole career given support to such arguments
by his conduct. But yet he has never in truth been
a clergyman. Though an ordained priest, he has
done no priestly work, and has always been somewhat angry when any one has suggested to him that
he should take a part in any clerical duties. At
first, indeed, he was somewhat careful in maintaining
outward clerical symbols, and was occasionally anx-
ious to feed himself with inward clerical thoughts,
having been moved thereto by the terrible earnestness of his ordination,—by the solemnity of a ceremony which, though he had determined to regard it
simply as the means of placing him in the possession
of certain temporal advantages, so impressed itself
upon him as being personal to himself, that he could
not at once escape from its bonds. But gradually
he overcame that weakness, and found himself

enabled to live, as any other gentleman might live, an easy pleasant life, with nothing of the clergyman about him but the word Reverend attached to his name on his cards and letters. The colour of his lower vestments approaches perhaps nearer to black than it would have done had he not been so encumbered, and men in the world at large are perhaps a little less free in their remarks before him than they would be before other men. This he regrets painfully; but it is all that he has to regret. The fellows, his predecessors in the old days,—who were, in fact, monks as well as fellows,—were called upon to live in accordance with certain monastic and ascetic rules, which they either obeyed to their supposed glory, or disobeyed to their supposed peril. Matins, lauds, nones, vespers, complines, and what not, were their lot,—and came upon them heavily enough, no doubt, if they did their duty ; but now-a-days we do not care much, even at our universities, for lauds and complines. Undergraduates indeed must " keep " so many chapels a week, but the clerical fellow is under no such bond. Even if he were under such bond he could say his prayers in his college chapel as well as a layman as he can as a clergyman. And one may suppose that as a layman he would abstain from doing so when the opportunity is provided with an easier conscience than he can have as a priest. But his conscience is easy, because he knows that in fact he is no clergyman. He has simply undergone a certain ceremony in order that he may enjoy his fellowship,—and hereafter take a living should the amiable and tender relationship of matrimony fall in his way.

VIII.

THE CURATE IN A POPULOUS PARISH.

Would that it were possible to enforce upon the bishops, as a part of their duty, the task of furnishing annually a statistical return which should show what proportion of the clerical duties in their dioceses was done by curates, and what proportion by other clergymen ; and also what payment had been made to the curates for the work so done, and what payment to those who were not curates. Such statement might show us for instance, in a tabulated form, how many morning services and how many evening services had been performed by each curate, how many sermons preached by him, how many children baptized, how many dead men buried, how many marriages celebrated, and, above all, how many cottages visited.

Then, if we could see, together with all this, what
amount of the payment received could be justly
appropriated to each task performed, we should have
some clear idea of the manner in which the revenues
of the Church are divided among those who do the
work of the Church. We all know that no such
statistical information is within our reach. The
bishops are altogether beyond our power, and cannot be ordered by any one to do anything. The
idea of comparing the work done with the payment
given for the work would be horrible to the imagination of every beneficed clergyman in the Church of
England. It would be horrible even to the imagination of the curates themselves, who, like the needy
knifegrinder, have no adequate conception of the injustice they are themselves suffering; and who are,
as a body, so well inclined towards the rules and
traditions of the profession to which they belong,
that they have not as yet taught themselves to wish
for a change. No clergyman in our Church has, as
yet, taken it into his head that there should be any
analogy, or any proportion, between work and wages
in his profession, as there is such analogy and such

proportion in all other professions. There is a something of revolutionary tendency in the suggestion that clergymen should be paid in accordance with their work, which is almost profane to the mind of a clergyman, and which vexes him sorely as being subversive of that grand position which he holds as the owner of a temporal freehold. The very irregularity of the payments still made to parish parsons, and formerly made to bishops, half justifies a latent idea that clergymen, though they work and receive payment, are not labourers working for hire. A second son inherits his living as the elder son inherits his estate;—and the rector who receives his living from his bishop is equally firm in his possession. He may be blessed with 1,000*l.* a year for doing very little, or have 200*l.* a year for doing a great deal; but in either case what he receives has no connection with what he does, and therefore no such statistics as those of which we have spoken can be supplied. No revelation will be made to us tending in any degree to give us the information for which we ask.

That there will come an adjustment between work and wages in the Church, as in all other professions,

is certain.   Indeed, much has been done towards this
adjustment already, though not after the fashion
above proposed.   The incomes of all bishops have
been arranged on such an idea,—to the great detri-
ment, as has before been explained, of episcopal
magnificence.   Deans and canons have fallen beneath
the levelling hands of ecclesiastico-political econo-
mists.   And out of the funds which have been
acquired by these adjustments and curtailings of
ecclesiastical wealth, certain incumbents working in
populous parishes have received augmentations of
pay, making their incomes up to the very modest
stipend of 300*l*. per annum.   But nothing in all
this has touched the great body of the clergymen
of the Church of England, or has as yet shown
any general recognition of the principle that the
hire of the labourer should be proportioned to the
labour done.

In speaking of the work and wages of curates, it
must of course be admitted that in all professions
and all trades the beginner should be contented to
work his way up, taking at first, and being contented
to take, a modest remuneration for the very best that

he can do. The young barrister does not get fifty-guinea fees at once, nor does the young medical practitioner jump at once into the good graces of the old ladies and gentlemen who make the fortunes of mature doctors ; but at the bar, and in the profession of physic, there is at least some proportion kept. The man who gets the most money is generally the hardest-worked man ;—or if, in some cases, it be not so, the lower man who works harder than him above him receives something like a fair share of the spoil. If he be successful in work he is successful in pay also. Being successful in work, he will not work without success in pay. But the curate, let his success in work be what it may, does not even think that he has, on that account, a claim to proportionate remuneration. If he can get to the soft side of his bishop, if he have an aunt that knows some friend of the Lord Chancellor, or a father who has means to buy a living for him,—and he be not himself of too tender a conscience in the matter of simony,— then he may hope to rise. But of rising in his profession because he is fit to rise he has no hope. The idea has not, as yet, come home to him that he has a positive claim upon his bishop because he has worked hard and honestly in his profession.

It is notorious that a rector in the Church of England, in the possession of a living of, let us say, a thousand a year, shall employ a curate at seventy pounds a year, that the curate shall do three-fourths or more of the work of the parish, that he shall remain in that position for twenty years, taking one-fourteenth of the wages while he does three-fourths of the work, and that nobody shall think that the rector is wrong or the curate ill-used! All the world,—that is to say, the rector's friends and the curate's friends also,—have been so long accustomed to this state of things, the bishops have had it so long under their eyes, the idea of a temporal free-hold in a living being a good thing for the parson instead of a good thing for the parishioner has got such a hold of us all,—that we none of us see the injustice of the present practice, or stop to inquire how it grew up among us, originating in a practice that was not unjust. When the rectors and vicars were very many among us in comparison to the curates, when a curate was needed in but few parishes,

—the ordinary tenure of a curacy was, of course, short. There have been instances, no doubt, since the earliest years in which curates were employed, of curates who have remained curates till they were old men ; but the succession from the smaller number of the inferior grade to the much larger number of the superior grade was, of course, rapid, and a clerical babe would be contented to take a curacy even at seventy pounds a year, who might reasonably expect to be raised from that humble position after a service of two or three years. But now-a-days, since the immense increase of population has forced upon us an increase of curates,—any increase in the number of endowed rectors and vicars being out of our reach, —the clerical babe must become a clerical old man on the same pittance, and it is coming to pass that young men whose friends have been at the trouble of giving them a good education, do not like the prospect of becoming curates, without any prospect of rising from their curacies to the glories and comforts of full-blown parsondom.

And in considering this matter we must remember that the curate of to-day is deprived of a great advan-

tage which belonged as a matter of course to the
curate of yesterday. The latter was presumed to be,
by virtue of his calling, a gentleman, and as such
possessed almost a right to be admitted into society
which neither his fortune nor his own abilities would
have opened to him. He was a gentleman as it were
by Act of Parliament, and it was understood that he
might receive where he could not give, and so enjoy
many of those good things which a liberal income
produces, though such things were beyond the reach
of his own purse. Thus the pains of his position
were mitigated. And in this way the poor clergyman
mixed with men who were not poor, and received
a something from his status in the world, to which
no disgrace was attached, though it was something
which he could not return. But we may say that all
this is now altered. A clergyman is no longer a
gentleman by Act of Parliament. Till the other day
he was admitted into all families simply because he
had a place in the reading-desk of the parish church ;
—but he is no longer so admitted. Things have
become changed within a few years, and mothers are
becoming as chary of admitting the curate among their

flocks—till they know exactly what are the curate's bearings—as they have ever been in regard to the new young doctor till they have known his bearings. Under these circumstances, all men who care for the Church of England are beginning to ask themselves how the race of curates is to be continued.

Let us for a moment look at the life of a curate of the present day. We will suppose that he comes from some college at Cambridge or Oxford. We will so suppose because Cambridge and Oxford still give us the majority of our clergymen, though we can hardly hope that they will long continue to be so bountiful. He enters the Church, moved to do so by what we all call a special vocation. During the period of his education he feels himself to be warmed towards the teaching of the English Protestant Church, and as he finds the ministry easily in his way he enters it—and at about the age of twenty-four he becomes a curate. He is at first gratified at the ease with which are confided to him the duties of an assistant in the cure of souls, and does not think much of the stipend which is allotted to him. He has lived as a boy at the university upon two hundred

a year without falling much into debt, and thinks
that as a man he can live easily upon seventy pounds.
Hitherto he has indulged himself with many things.
He has smoked cigars, and had his wine parties, and
been luxurious ; but as a curate he will be delighted
to deny himself all luxuries.   His heart will be in
the service of his God, and his appetites shall be to
him as thorns which he will make to crackle in the
fire.   To eat bread without butter and to drink tea
without milk is a glory to him,— and so he begins
the world.

And for a year or two, if he be not weak-minded,
things do not go badly with him.   The parson's wife
sees far into his character, and is kind to him, stirred
thereto by a conviction of which she is herself unconscious, that the money payment made by her
husband is insufficient.   The dry bread and the
brown tea are still sweetened by reminiscences of St.
Paul's sufferings, and the young man consoles himself by inward whisperings of forty stripes save one
five times repeated.   To be persecuted is as yet sweet
to him, and he knows that in doing all the rector's
work for seventy pounds a year he is being per-

secuted.   But anon there grows up within his breast
a feeling in which the grievance as regards this world
is brought into unpleasant contact with the persecu-
tion in which he has a pietistic delight.   He still
rejoices in the reflection that he cannot possibly buy
for himself a much-needed half-dozen of new shirts,
but is uncomfortably angry because the rector himself
is not only idle, but has bought a new carriage.
And then he gives way a little—the least in the
world—and at the end of the year owes the butcher
a small bill which he cannot settle.   From that day
the vision of St. Paul melts before his eyes, and he
sighs for replenished fleshpots.

But he still works hard in his curacy,—perhaps
harder than ever, driven thereto by certain inward
furies.   What will become of him,—of him, with his
seventy pounds a year, and nothing further to expect
as professional result, if he be deserted by his religious ecstasy ?   But religious ecstasy will not permit
itself to be maintained on such terms, and gradually
there creeps upon him the heart-breaking disappoint-
ment of a soured and an injured man.   In the midst
of this he takes to himself a wife.   It is always so.

The man who is most in the dark will be the best inclined to take a leap in the dark. In the lowest period of his despondency he becomes a married man —enjoying at the moment a little fitful gleam of shortlived worldly pleasure. Then, again, he is a male saint for a few months, with a female saint beside him ; and after that all collapses, and he goes down into irrevocable misery and distress. In a few years we know of him as a beggar of old clothes, as a man whom from time to time his friends are asked to lift from unutterable depths of distress by donations which no gentleman can take without a crushed spirit—as a pauper whom the poor around him know to be a pauper, and will not, therefore, respect as a minister of their religion. In all this there has been very little, we may say nothing, of fault in the curate himself. As a young man, almost as a boy, he placed himself in a position of which he knew the old conditions rather than those then existing around him—and through that mistake he fell.

But young men are now beginning to know, and the fathers of young men also, what are at present the true conditions of the Church of England as a profession, and they who have been nurtured softly, and who have any choice, will not undergo its trials —and its injustice! For men of a lower class in life, who have come from harder antecedents, the normal seventy pounds per annum may suffice; but all modern Churchmen will understand what must be the effect on the Church if such be the recruits to which the Church must trust.

IX.

THE IRISH BENEFICED CLERGYMAN.

THE difference between an Irish and an English parson is greater, perhaps, than that which exists between Irishmen and Englishmen of any other special denomination, and is of a nature exactly contrary to that which generally marks the distinctive character of the Milesian and the John Bull. The normal Irishman is a jolly fellow; but the normal Irish Protestant clergyman is a severe, sombre man, one who speaks of life in sad, subdued tones,—unless when he is minatory in the pulpit,—one who looks at things around him with a continual remembrance that life is but a span long, that men are but grass of the field, that the sickle is ready and the oven heated, and that it is worth no man's while to be comfortable here on earth. He is preaching every moment of his life, preaching in his gait, preaching in every tone of his voice, preaching in every act that he does, preaching in every turn of his eyes. Find him asleep, and you will find him preaching with a long-protracted, indignant, low-church, Protestant snore, very eloquent as to the scarlet woman. But an English parson, let him be ever so much given to preaching, preaches only from his pulpit. He may scold, advise, or cajole in the school, the cottage, or the drawing-room ; but he keeps his sermons for his Sunday work. An Irish clergyman does not shake hands with you without leaving a text or two in your palm,—with his own special comments on their tenour as regards the Pope.

The reason of this is not far to seek. The Irish clergyman does not live in the midst of Protestants with whom he sympathizes, but is surrounded by Roman Catholics with whom he cannot sympathize, and against whom he is driven to feel almost a personal enmity, not only by reason of their creed which he sorely hates, but by reason also of the anomalies of his own position which are so hateful to them. He is always in a state of feud,—in a state

of feud, not only against the devil, as should be the
case with all of us whether clergymen or laymen, but
against Antichrist on the Seven Hills, against the
scarlet woman who goes about devouring, against the
Pope who is to him a ravenous old woman as to whom
he cannot say whether he is most ravenous or most
old-womanish, against a creed which has for him
none of the attractions of Christianity,—in which he
sees only the small points of divergence from his own,
and which is, therefore, worse to him than the creed
of Mussulman or of Jew. He is therefore always
serious, as is a soldier who is ever buckling on his
armour, and somewhat sad, as is a soldier who cannot
get his enemy down so that he may take away his
standard and trample on him. The Irish Protestant
clergyman is ever longing to lead troops of the Roman
Catholics of Ireland in triumph to the top of the
Tarpeian rock of conversion ; but they succeed in
bringing thither but one and another, and these one
and another are such that they hardly grace the
chariot wheels of their victors.

The popular idea of an Irish clergyman in
England is, we think, somewhat incorrect. He is

often supposed to be an idle man, listless for want of occupation, given to self-indulgence, ill-educated, eager only in defence of his temporalities, and warmly attached to the party politics of Protestants, rather than to their religion. Such men may doubtless be found among the holders of livings in Ireland, as they may also in England; but such is not the general character of the Irish clergyman. He is a man always active, though unfortunately his activity has but small field of usefulness. His air is not the air of a listless man, but of a man disappointed,—as it may well be. As he goes on in life he may come to love too dearly his slippers and his armchair, and perhaps to feel, as disappointed men will feel,—will feel but not acknowledge,—that the consolations of the dinner-table are, and that none others are, reliable; but such is not his normal condition of body or mind. I will not say that he is generally well-educated,—because the word means so much. But the Irish clergyman has generally read as much as his brother in England, though his reading has been of a different nature. Of reading applicable specially to his own profession he has probably endured more than his brother in England. In short he is more of a clergyman and less of a man of the world than the English parson,—with this misfortune, that his clerical activities are always at work against enemies and not on behalf of friends.

There would not be space for me to say much, in this short sketch, of the now acknowledged anomalies of the position of the Church of England as established in Ireland; but I will endeavour to describe the outward form and bearing of the clergyman whom these anomalies have produced, begging my readers to believe at the outset that the Irish clergyman may be regarded, nine times out of ten,—ninety-nine out of a hundred I think we might say,—as a sincere man, as a man with strong convictions, who has no shadow of doubt in his own mind that the surest road to heaven, if not the only one, is by that special pathway of which he professes to have the clue. There is no reservation within his mind, as to his religion with its intricacies being good for the ignorant, for instance, though perhaps not altogether needed for the educated. He has no doubts. The Eureka with him is a certainty. That men will be saved and will be damned as they live remote from or attached to papistical teachings is to him a reality. Now it is something that a man should be capable of a sincere belief, and that he should succeed in attaining to it.

The Irish beneficed clergyman has almost always been educated at Trinity, Dublin, and has there been indoctrinated with those high Protestant principles with which he has before been inoculated. He is, of course, the son of an Irish Protestant gentleman, and has therefore sucked them in with his mother's milk. He goes before his Protestant bishop and takes his orders with a corps of other young men exactly similarly circumstanced. And thus he has never had given to him an opportunity of rubbing his own ideas against those of men who have been educated with different proclivities. He has never lived at college either with Roman Catholics, or with Presbyterians, or with Protestants of a sort different from his sort. In his cradle, at his father's table, at school, at the university, in all the lessons that he has learned, in all the games that he has played, in his converse with his sisters, in his first soft, faint, whisperings with his sisters' friends, in his loud unreserved talkings with his closest companions, the same two ideas, cheek by jowl, have ever been present to him,— the State ascendancy of his own Church, and the numerical superiority of another Church antagonistic to his own. When we consider all this, and look at the training which the Irish clergyman has undergone, how can we wonder at his idiosyncrasies?

Irish clergymen are thus bound together more closely than clergymen in England, chiefly from the want of opportunity for divergence. Not only education goes always in the same course, but the circumstances of professional career attach themselves very closely to one form. The livings are more generally in the gift of the bishops than with us, and the Irish bishops, perhaps, are more inclined to give promotion solely on the score of merit than are the English bishops. There is, we believe, less of Church patronage,—or rather of the exercise of Church patronage for the furthering of private ends; and if this be so, the Irish Church in that respect is superior to our own. But as the Irish curate is to get his living from the Irish bishop, and is to receive

it as a reward for his clerical zeal, and not because he
is his father's son, it is absolutely incumbent on him
to work as a curate up to the established diocesan
mark.   And this mark or standard will not be the
standard fixed exactly by the bishop himself. Bishop's
predecessors and bishop's chaplains, and the very air
round the bishop's residence, will have been for years
impregnated with high Protestant principles.   And
even a bishop who may himself be lacking in that
fiery Protestant zeal which is regarded as Church of
England orthodoxy in Ireland, will not find himself
able to subdue the strength of the atmosphere in
which he is called upon to live.   There have been
bishops sent to Ireland,—nay, there still are bishops
in Ireland, placed over dioceses there because they
have been considered to be,—we will not say anti-
Protestant, but liberal in their tendencies towards
Roman Catholics and Presbyterians ; but the clergymen who come forth ordained from under the hands
of the liberal Whatelys are nearly of the same form
as those who, from time out of mind, have been given
to us by the orthodox Trenches and the orthodox
Beresfords.   The stream runs too strongly to be

stemmed by any bishop;—so that the Irish clergyman
who desires to swim must, almost of necessity, swim
with it.

The clerical aspirant becomes first a curate. One
would be disposed to think that there could be no
great need for curates in Ireland,—that as the population of the country is chiefly Roman Catholic, and
as not much above one-half even of the Protestants
conforms to the Church of England,—so that the
proportion of even nominal church-goers is less than
one in eight,—and as there is a beneficed parson in
every parish, whether there be much, little, or nothing
to do,—curates could not be needed in addition to
rectors and vicars ; but curates seem to be as common
in Ireland as they are in England,—the souls of men
requiring, we must suppose, more surveillance, and
the work, we must presume, being more closely done.
The young clergyman almost always becomes a curate,
and then looks to his bishop for a living. Depending
thus on the bishop, he lives strictly, works with
energy, is constant in his adherence to all the exigen-
cies of his cloth, and in the ripeness of time is blessed
with a living of, we will say, two hundred and fifty

pounds a year with a glebe. Irish livings are thought
to be very good, but the value here named is above
the average. In the rich diocese of Meath, perhaps
of all the Irish dioceses the richest, the endowment of
more than one-half of the livings is less than the sum
above named. Then begins the real battle of his life.
Of course our Irish clergyman marries, and of course
he has a family, and, even in Ireland, the support of
a wife and family upon two hundred and fifty pounds
a year is not easy. His glebe is probably remote
from any town, and far removed from the houses of
other gentry. The parish squire is a personage who,
as such, hardly exists in Ireland. Here and there a
resident landowner is to be found with a large house
and a wide demesne ; but the parish squire who has
interests in the parish almost identical with those of
the parson does not exist. The clergyman, therefore,
located in the country lives alone, and his nearest
neighbours are the rectors and vicars of other parishes.
He lives alone, and the solitude of his life does not
tend to make him jovial, or even satisfied with things
around him. But he has his religion, and he tells
himself that that should suffice for him ;—that that

should be all in all to him. He has his religion, and he endeavours to make the most of it. It is to be not only his guide through life to things spiritual, but his chief comfort in things temporal. He must abide by it in every phase under which it has been presented to him ; he must hang to it as the politician does to his party ; he must trust to it,—not merely for the God and Saviour whom he knows through its assistance, but for his very politics, thoroughly believing that all its doctrines and all its formularies are essentially necessary, and that they must be taken with the exact tenets and with all the twists which have been given to them by his side in church disputes.

Of all men the Irish beneficed clergyman is the most illiberal, the most bigoted, the most unforgiving, the most sincere, and the most enthusiastic. He is too often an unhappy man, being poor, aggrieved, soured by the misfortunes of his own position, conscious that something is wrong, though never doubting that he himself is right, aware of his own unavoidable idleness, aware that when he works he works to little or no effect, feeling that prayers said and sermons preached to his own family, to three policemen and his clerk, cannot be said to have been preached to much effect. It is a life-long grief to him that in his parish there should be four hundred and fifty nominal Roman Catholics, and only fifty nominal members of the Church of England. But yet he is staunch. There is a good day coming, though he will never see it. He consoles himself as best he may with the certainty of the coming triumph; but cannot refrain from sadness as he tells himself that it certainly will not come in his days.

There is nothing more melancholy to a man's heart, nothing more depressing to his feelings, than a doubt whether or no he truly earns the bread which he eats. The beneficed clergyman of the Church of England in Ireland has no doubt as to his right to his bread,—as to his right either by the law of man or by the law of God ; but he cannot but have a doubt as to his earning it. He tells himself that it is the fault of the people,—that it comes of their darkness ; that he is there if they will only come to him. But they do not come ; and he has on his spirit the terrible weight of wages received without adequate work performed. It is a killing weight.

To preach to three policemen is as hard as to preach to three hundred educated men and women,—nay, perhaps it is much harder; but he who so preaches feels that his preaching is nothing. He is as the convict labourer who moves sand from one hole to another;—and who can get no comfort from his work.

And he is daily told,—this Irish beneficed clergyman of the Church of England,—that of all men he is the most overpaid. Newspapers which he cannot but see, speakers on public platforms to whose orations he cannot entirely stop his ears, are telling him constantly that he is a drone, growing fat upon honey which he does not help to make, threatening him with Parliamentary annihilation, and invoking against him all the ardour of all the Radicals. In the meantime, he knows that he and his are barely able to subsist on the pittance which the Church allows him. He has terrible temporal grievances in poor rates, charges for his glebe, deductions on this side and on that, till he knows not how to pay his butcher and his baker, and the wife of his bosom is driven to painful, stringent economies. He has not, he tells himself, half of that which a liberal Church in old days had intended for the parish, and yet they tell him that he is robbing the public ! He is there to do his duty. Why do not the people come to him ? For what he receives, whether it is much or little, he is ready to work, if only his work might be accepted.

But his work is not accepted, and there is no slightest sign in Ireland that it will be accepted. The anomalies of the Church of England in Ireland are terribly distressing, and call aloud for reform. But to none can they be so distressing as to the beneficed clergyman in Ireland ; and in the behalf of no other class is that reform so vitally needed.

X. AND LAST.

THE CLERGYMAN WHO SUBSCRIBES FOR COLENSO.

WE have heard much of the Broad Church for many years, till the designation is almost as familiar to our ears as that of the High Church or of the Low Church ; but the Broad Church of former times,— some twenty years ago, we will say, when the ecclesiastical world was all on fire because the then Prime Minister was minded to give a mitre to a certain professor of divinity at Oxford,—held doctrines very far indeed behind those to which the liberal parsons of these days have made progress. The ordinary Broad Church clergyman of that era was one who showed himself to be broad by his tolerance of the doubts of others, rather than by the expression of doubts of his own. He was not uncomfortably shocked at finding himself in company with one who was weak in faith as to the Old Testament miracles, and listened with placid equanimity to discussions which went on around him to show that our ancient Bible chronology was defective. But now we have got much beyond that. The liberal clergyman of the Church of England has long since given up Bible chronology, has given up many of the miracles, and is venturing forward into questions the very asking of which would have made the hairs to stand on end on the head of the broadest of the broad in the old days, twenty years since. There are bishops still living, and others have lately died, who must have been astonished to find how quickly their teaching has had its results, how soon the tree has produced its fruit.

The free-thinking clergyman of the present time is to be found more often in London than in the provinces, and more frequently in the towns than in country parishes. They are not many in number, as compared with the numbers of all parsondom in these realms; but they are men of whom we hear much, and they are sufficiently numerous to leaven the whole. There are many things, gone recently altogether out of date, which the meek old-world clergyman dares no longer teach, though he knows not why,—the placid, easy-minded clergyman who would be so well satisfied to teach all that his father taught before him,—the actual six days for instance, the actual and needed rest on the seventh; but the placid clergyman dares not teach them, not knowing why he dares not. He has been leavened unconsciously by the free-thinking of his liberal brother, and his teaching comes forth conformed in some degree to the new doctrines, although, to himself, the feeling is simply that the ground is being cut from under him, and that that special bit of ground, —the actual six days, has slid away altogether from the touch of his feet.

In London and in the large towns, where they most abound, these new teachers have their own circles, their own flocks, their own churches, and their admirers who have become familiar with them. And it is when so placed, no doubt, that they are most efficacious in operating on the education of laymen and of other clergymen. But it is when such a one finds himself placed as a parson in a country parish, out, as it were, alone among the things of another day, that he calls upon himself the greatest attention.   He has around him antediluvian rectors and pietistic vicars, who regard him not only as a bird of prey who has got into a community of domestic poultry, but, worse still, as a bird that is fouling its own nest.   They hate his teaching, as all teachers must hate doctrines which are subversive of their own—which, however, they can themselves neither subvert nor approve.   But they hate more intensely that want of professional thoroughness, that absence of esprit de corps, which these gentlemen seem to them to exhibit.   "He has taken orders," says the antediluvian rector, speaking of his free-thinking neighbour to his confidential friend, " simply to upset the Church !   He believes in nothing ; nothing in heaven, nothing on earth,—nothing under the earth.   He told his people yesterday that the Book of Exodus is an old woman's story.   And the worst of it is, we cannot do anything to get rid of him ;—no, by Heaven, not anything ! "   To which the rector's confidential friend replies that the rector

has still the power left of preaching his own doctrine.
" Psha ! " says the rector, " preach, indeed ! Preach
the Devil as he does, and you can fill a church any
day ! What I want to know is how a man like that
can bring himself to take four hundred a year out of
the Church, when he doesn't believe one of the
Articles he has sworn to ? " Now the special offence
of the liberal preacher on this occasion was a hint
conveyed in a sermon that the fourth commandment
in its entirety is hardly compatible with the life of
an Englishman in the nineteenth century. And the
laymen around are astounded by the man, feeling a
great interest in him, not unmixed with awe. Has
he come to them from Heaven or from Hell? Are
these new teachings, which are not without their
comfort, promptings direct from the Evil One, who
is ever roaring for their souls, and who may thus
have come to roar in their own parish ? There is
mystery as well as danger in the matter; and as
mystery, and danger also when not too near, are both
pleasant, the new man is not altogether unwelcome,
in spite of the anathemas of the neighbouring rector.
What if the new teaching should be true ? So the

men begin to speculate, and the women quake, and the neighbouring parsons are full of wrath, and the bishop's table groans with letters which he knows not how to answer, or how to leave unanswered. The free-thinking clergyman of whom we are speaking still creates much of this excitement in the country; but in the town he is encountered on easier terms, and in London he finds his own set, and has no special weight beyond that which his talents and his energy can give him.

It is very hard to come at the actual belief of any man. Indeed how should we hope to do so when we find it so very hard to come at our own? How many are there among us who, in this matter of our religion, which of all things is the most important to us, could take pen in hand and write down even for their own information exactly what they themselves believe? Not very many clergymen even, if so pressed, would insert boldly and plainly the fulminating clause of the Athanasian Creed; and yet each clergyman declares aloud that he believes it a dozen times every year of his life. Most men who call themselves Christians would say that they believed

the Bible, not knowing what they meant, never
having attempted,—and very wisely having refrained
from attempting amidst the multiplicity of their
worldly concerns,—to separate historical record from
inspired teaching. But when a liberal-minded clergyman does come among us,—come among us, that is,
as our pastor,—we feel not unnaturally a desire to
know what it is, at any rate, that he disbelieves. On
what is he unsound, according to the orthodoxy of
our old friend the neighbouring rector ? And are we
prepared to be unsound with him ? We know that
there are some things which we do not like in the
teaching to which we have been hitherto subjected ;—
that fulminating clause, for instance, which tells us
that nobody can be saved unless he believes a great
deal which we find it impossible to understand ; the
ceremonial Sabbath which we know that we do not
observe, though we go on professing that its observ-
ance is a thing necessary for us ;—the incompatibility
of the teaching of Old Testament records with the
new teachings of the rocks and stones. Is it within
our power to get over our difficulties by squaring our
belief with that of this new parson whom we acknow-

ledge at any rate to be a clever fellow ? Before we
can do so we must at any rate know what is the
belief,—or the unbelief,—that he has in him.

But this is exactly what we never can do. The
old rector was ready enough with his belief. There
were the three creeds, and the thirty-nine articles ;
and, above all, there was the Bible,—to be taken
entire, unmutilated, and unquestioned. His task
was easy enough, and he believed that he believed
what he said that he believed. But the new parson
has by no means so glib an answer ready to such a
question. He is not ready with his answer because
he is ever thinking of it. The other man was ready
because he did not think. Our new friend, however,
is debonair and pleasant to us, with something of a
subrisive smile in which we rather feel than know
that there is a touch of irony latent. The question
asked troubles him inwardly, but he is well aware
that he should show no outward trouble. So he is
debonair and kind,—still with that subrisive smile,—
and bids us say our prayers, and love our God, and
trust our Saviour. The advice is good, but still we
want to know whether we are to pray God to help us

to keep the Fourth Commandment, or only pretend
so to pray,—and whether, when the fulminating
clause is used, we are to try to believe it or to
disbelieve it. We can only observe our new rector,
and find out from his words and his acts how his own
mind works on these subjects.

It is soon manifest to us that he has accepted the
teaching of the rocks and stones, and that we may
give up the actual six days, and give up also the
deluge as a drowning of all the world. Indeed, we
had almost come to fancy that even the old rector
had become hazy on these points. And gradually
there leak out to us, as to the falling of manna from
heaven, and as to the position of Jonah within the
whale, and as to the speaking of Balaam's ass, certain
doubts, not expressed indeed, but which are made
manifest to us as existing by the absence of expres-
sions of belief. In the intercourse of social life we
see something of a smile cross our new friend's face
when the thirty-nine articles are brought down beneath his nose. Then he has read the *Essays and
Reviews*, and will not declare his opinion that the
writers of them should be unfrocked and sent away

into chaos ;—nay, we find that he is on terms of personal intimacy with one at least among the number of those writers. And, lastly, there comes out a subscription list for Bishop Colenso, and we find our new rector's name down for a five-pound note ! That we regard as the sign, to be recognized by us as the most certain of all signs, that he has cut the rope which bound his barque to the old shore, and that he is going out to sea in quest of a better land. Shall we go with him, or shall we stay where we are ?

If one could stay, if one could only have a choice in the matter, if one could really believe that the old shore is best, who would leave it ? Who would not wish to be secure if he knew where security lay ? But this new teacher, who has come among us with his ill-defined doctrines and his subrisive smile,—he and they who have taught him,—have made it impossible for us to stay. With hands outstretched towards the old places, with sorrowing hearts,—with hearts which still love the old teachings which the mind will no longer accept,—we, too, cut our ropes, and go out in our little boats, and search for a land that will be new to us, though how far new,—new in how many things, we do not know. Who would not stay behind if it were possible to him?

But our business at present is with the teacher, and not with the taught. Of him we may declare that he is, almost always, a true man,—true in spite of that subrisive smile and ill-defined doctrine. He is one who, without believing, cannot bring himself to think that he believes, or to say that he believes that which he disbelieves without grievous suffering to himself. He has to say it, and does suffer. There are the formulas which must be repeated, or he must abandon his ministry altogether,—his ministry, and his adopted work, and the public utility which it is his ambition to achieve. Debonair though he be, and smile though he may, he has through it all some terrible heart-struggles, in which he is often tempted to give way and to acknowledge that he is too weak for the work he has taken in hand. When he resolved that he must give that five pounds to the Colenso fund,—or rather when he resolved that he must have his name printed in the public list, for an anonymous giving of his money would have been nothing,—he knew that his rope was indeed cut, and that his boat was in truth upon the wide waters. After that it will serve him little to say that such an act on his part implies no agreement with the teaching of the African bishop. He had, by the subscription, attached himself to the Broad Church with the newest broad principles, and must expect henceforth to be regarded as little better than an infidel,—certainly as an enemy in the camp, — by the majority of his brethren of the day. "Why does he not give up his tithes? Why does he stick to his temporalities?" says the old-fashioned, wrathful parson of the neighbouring parish; and the sneer, which is repeated from day to day and from month to month, is not slow to reach the new man's ear. It is an accusation hard to be borne; but it has to be borne,—among other things,—by the clergyman who subscribes for Colenso.

THE END.